the To&Through project

UCHICAGO Consortium on School Research

I0165842

RESEARCH REPORT   OCTOBER 2017

Patterns of Two-Year and Four-Year College Enrollment Among Chicago Public Schools Graduates

Vanessa M. Coca, Jenny Nagaoka, and Alex Seeskin

TABLE OF CONTENTS

The To&Through Project is a partnership between the University of Chicago's Urban Education Institute and the Network for College Success. The Project's mission is to use research, data, and professional learning to help more students get to and through high school and college:

- Research that illuminates what matters most for students' high school and college success
- Data that guides efforts to improve students' attainment of key milestones
- Professional Learning that helps translate research and data into improved practice

In collaboration with educators, policymakers, and communities, the To&Through Project aims to significantly increase the percentage of Chicago Public Schools freshmen who graduate from high school and go on to earn a college degree, and to share the learning from Chicago with education stakeholders across the country.

ACKNOWLEDGEMENTS

The authors gratefully acknowledge the many people who contributed to this report. The content of this report was shaped by valuable feedback provided by the To&Through Community College advisory board and other members of the Chicago education community. Consortium Steering Committee members Alan Mather, Shazia Miller, and Paige Ponder offered very thoughtful reviews as we finalized the narrative. We thank the members of the UChicago Consortium's research review group, particularly Elaine Allensworth, Kylie Klein, and Lauren Sartain, as well as our external reviewers, Eliza Moeller and Will Torres, and our technical reviewer, Julia Gwynne, for their helpful feedback. Members of the UChicago Consortium's communications team, including Bronwyn McDaniel, Jessica Tansey, and Jessica Puller, were instrumental in the production of this report. We also thank Melissa Roderick and the UChicago Consortium's post-secondary research team for providing the research base that guides this report.

This work was supported by the Crown Family Philanthropies. We thank them for their support and collaboration with this project. The UChicago Consortium greatly appreciates support from the Consortium Investor Council that funds critical work beyond the initial research: putting the research to work, refreshing the data archive, seeding new studies, and replicating previous studies. Members include: Brinson Family Foundation, CME Group Foundation, Crown Family Philanthropies, Lloyd A. Fry Foundation, Joyce Foundation, Lewis-Sebring Family Foundation, McCormick Foundation, McDougal Family Foundation, Osa Family Foundation, Polk Bros. Foundation, Spencer Foundation, Steans Family Foundation, and The Chicago Public Education Fund.

Cite as: Coca, V.M., Nagaoka, J., & Seeskin, A. (2017). *Patterns of two-year and four-year college enrollment among Chicago Public Schools graduates.* Chicago, IL: University of Chicago Consortium on School Research.

This report was produced by the UChicago Consortium's publications and communications staff: Bronwyn McDaniel, Director of Outreach and Communication; Jessica Tansey, Communications Manager; Jessica Puller, Communications Specialist; and R. Steven Quispe, Development and Communications Coordinator.

Graphic Design: Jeff Hall Design
Photography: Eileen Ryan
Editing: Jessica Puller, Ann Linder, and Jessica Tansey

10.2017/pdf/jh.design@rcn.com

Introduction

A high school diploma is no longer seen as an economically viable terminal degree. The expectation now is that high school graduates will take the next step of enrolling in college and ultimately attain a post-secondary degree or credential. Chicago's high school graduates themselves share this expectation of needing to continue their education: 87 percent report planning to complete some form of post-secondary degree or certificate.[1]

This report takes a closer look at an essential milestone to a post-secondary credential—college enrollment— and provides a descriptive examination of the patterns among Chicago Public Schools (CPS) graduates over the last decade for both two-year colleges and four-year colleges, including a focus on 2015 graduates.[2]

School systems, community-based organizations, not-for-profit service providers, and institutions of higher education around the country, including CPS and City Colleges of Chicago (City Colleges), have prioritized helping students reach the critical milestone of enrollment.[3] CPS has set a goal that 60 percent of all its graduates complete a four-year degree by 2025, and has been a national leader in creating initiatives to support students in the transition to college.

At the two-year college level, City Colleges has engaged in efforts to "reinvent" their system. Since 2010, they have restructured and revamped program offerings (e.g., College to Careers), updated campus infrastructure, and provided scholarships for high-performing CPS

graduates (i.e., Chicago Star Scholarship[4]). As CPS, City Colleges, and higher education partners take on innovative efforts to improve college outcomes for CPS graduates, we need to assess recent trends on critical milestones, like enrollment, and to set a baseline for tracking the district's progress in the future.

Prior post-secondary work from the University of Chicago Consortium on School Research (UChicago Consortium) and the To&Through Project has focused on four-year colleges rather than two-year colleges. In this report, we examine the patterns of students who enroll in two-year and four-year colleges, and those who do not make the immediate transition to college. The inclusion of two-year colleges is important because national policy discussions increasingly emphasize the roles that two-year colleges can play in expanding access to higher education and in providing a viable path to a family-sustaining job.[5] Moreover, with rising tuition costs and changing financial aid options, equity of access to higher education for under-represented groups is a growing concern.

---

1 Results are based on responses to the 2016 *My Voice, My School* student survey administered to CPS seniors. In 2016, the high school response rate was 78 percent.
2 Throughout this report, the year refers to the spring of the school year; e.g. 2015 refers to the 2014–15 school year.
3 Other local initiatives include the Partnership for College Completion, Thrive Chicago's College Completion Change Network, and the Chicago Collaborative for Undergraduate Success.

4 In the spring of 2014, City Colleges announced their Star Scholarship—a merit-based scholarship that covers costs (including tuition and books) of attending any of the City Colleges for CPS graduates who have a 3.0 high school GPA or above, meet "college completion" benchmarks on the ACT or SAT, and enroll in an associate's degree program.
5 Carnevale, Jayasundera, & Hanson (2012).

This report provides a descriptive picture of college enrollment patterns to help policymakers and practitioners better understand which CPS graduates make the transition to college, and which students are in need of additional support. It highlights the college enrollment patterns among CPS graduates of different demographic and academic backgrounds, but does not seek to explain or identify the reasons for these patterns. Rather, this report lays the groundwork for future research on educational attainment by defining the current state of college enrollment among Chicago's students, and by showing how enrollment patterns have changed during a time of considerable shifts in the educational and economic landscape in Chicago. To help interpret the patterns, when possible, it provides national comparisons and describes related research findings. Additional details about district patterns and patterns by school are available on the To&Through Online Tool.[6]

Specifically, in this report we ask:

1. How has enrollment in two-year colleges and in four-year colleges changed over the last decade? (**Chapter 1**)

2. To what extent do the patterns of enrollment differ by racial/ethnic, socioeconomic, or academic background characteristics of students? To what extent do patterns vary by type of high school attended? (**Chapter 2**)

3. To what extent do enrollees at two-year colleges have academic qualifications that are different from enrollees at four-year colleges and from students who do not enroll in college? (**Chapter 3**)

The final section of this report provides implications for policy and practice, and identifies areas for future research to help guide current efforts to increase the educational attainment of CPS graduates in both two-year and four-year colleges.

---

6 For additional information please see toandthrough.uchicago.edu/tool

CHAPTER 1

Changes in College Enrollment Over the Last Decade

Chicago's Shifting Education Landscape

Over the last decade, Chicago's education landscape has changed in ways that could have influenced college participation, as well as shifted whether CPS graduates enrolled in two-year or four-year colleges. These changes include:

- Rising on-time high school graduation rates

- Continuing focus by CPS on college enrollment

- Shifting demographic composition of high school graduates

- Improving academic credentials of high school graduates

- Shifting national and local financial aid for post-secondary education

- Changing polices at the City Colleges of Chicago

- Growing number of non-profit organizations that support college access

Because several of these changes occurred simultaneously, studying the effect of any one change is challenging. Instead, in this section we briefly describe these changes and discuss how each might have shaped CPS graduates' trends in college enrollment rates within the last decade.

The most apparent change in the K-12 landscape has been the increase in on-time[7] high school graduation rates. The CPS graduation rate reached a record-high 74 percent in 2015.[8] This rapid rise in graduation rates has critical implications for the change in size and composition of the pool of potential college applicants. In fact, the increase in graduation rates has meant that the sheer number of high school graduates coming out of CPS has increased by more than 4,000 students between 2006 and 2015 (a 29 percent increase in the number of students). The post-secondary options of graduates, however, could be constrained by a number of factors. For example, enrollment rates could decrease if a larger proportion of students were graduating with low levels of preparation, if high schools did not strengthen their capacity to provide college counseling for this growing population, or if the number of seats in the most commonly attended post-secondary institutions did not grow at a similar rate. Taken together, these concerns beg the question: Has post-secondary enrollment kept pace with rising high school graduation rates?

District efforts to improve high school graduation rates have happened simultaneously with efforts to improve college enrollment rates. Since 2004, the district has organized its college access efforts through the Office of College and Career Success.[9] It was one of the first large school districts in the country to hold high schools responsible for supporting students in making post-secondary plans. Over the past decade, CPS has been a pioneer in district-led efforts to increase college enrollment, such as: building a data system to track FAFSA completion; creating college and career coach positions; including college enrollment and persistence rates in the accountability system; making college enrollment software available to all schools; and working with schools to develop post-secondary leadership teams.

The composition of the pool of high school graduates has also changed during this period, but in ways that make expectations of the direction of enrollment rates ambiguous. For example, the pool of potential first-time college freshmen is comprised of a growing share of

---

7   On-time graduation refers to whether a student attained a regular high school diploma within four years of starting high school. Unlike CPS, we do not include students who receive alternative diplomas or graduate from options high schools in our graduation numbers.

8   On-time high school graduation rates of CPS students have increased by 17 percentage points in the last decade (from 57 percent in 2006 to 74 percent in 2015; Nagaoka & Healey, 2016).

9   This office was originally called the Office of Post-Secondary Education and Student Development.

Latino students due to a larger number of Latino students entering CPS high schools, coupled with significant gains in the graduation rates of Latino students.[10] Prior research has found that Latino students were less likely to attend college than their similarly qualified peers[11] and more likely to attend two-year colleges when they do enroll.[12] Thus, given this shift in the demographic makeup of CPS graduates, we might expect rates of four-year college participation to stagnate or even to decrease, and for rates of two-year college enrollment to rise.

In addition to the changing demographics of CPS graduates, the academic qualifications of CPS graduates have improved over this period. Between 2006 and 2015, attendance rates, average ACT composite scores, the number of students taking AP coursework, and the percentage of students scoring a 3 or higher on an AP exam all increased.[13] Also, the percentage of graduates earning at least a 3.0 GPA increased from 21 percent in 2006 to 37 percent in 2015. These considerable improvements suggest that CPS's growing cohort of graduates are more academically prepared for college and, in turn, more likely to attend college and have greater access to a variety of post-secondary options than those who graduated more than a decade ago.

The local and national higher education financial landscapes have shifted over the last decade in ways that could have mixed effects on students' college enrollment patterns.[14] College costs have continued to rise. Published in-state tuition and fees at public four-year institutions increased at an average rate of 3.5 percent per year beyond inflation between 2006-07 and 2016-17, and 2.4 percent per year at non-profit, private four-year institutions.[15] Pell Grant awards, federal need-based grants, have also increased, with

the maximum award and the average award going up between 2006 and 2015. At the same time, the percentage of undergraduates qualifying for and receiving Pell Grants increased.[16] We would expect that these changes in federal aid may have mitigated the impact of rising college costs on college participation. Yet locally, the Illinois state-grant assistance program, Illinois Monetary Award Program (MAP), which was designed to make post-secondary enrollment more affordable for low-income students, has not been funded to keep up with rising post-secondary attendance and the rising cost of attendance. In 2012, only about half of MAP applicants received funding, and the maximum award covered only 37 percent of the average cost of tuition and fees at an Illinois public university.[17] These shifts in national and state funding for post-secondary education have serious repercussions for the post-secondary choices of CPS graduates, the vast majority of whom qualify for federal and state aid.[18]

More recently, due to state budget shortfalls in Illinois, MAP funding was severely delayed for the 2015-16 academic year. In response, some post-secondary institutions, particularly those serving a large share of MAP-eligible students, took drastic measures to temporarily cover funds that would have been provided by MAP grants (e.g., cutting faculty and staff positions; cutting programs and scholarships for students).[19] Because the most recent cohort of CPS graduates examined in this report is the 2015 cohort, we may not yet see the consequences of the budget shortfall for immediate enrollment rates. However, we might expect to see shifts in CPS graduates' post-secondary choices (e.g., overall enrollment and persistence) in the 2016-17 academic year.

---

10 Allensworth, Healey, Gwynne, & Crespin (2016a).

11 Klasik (2012); Roderick, Coca, & Nagaoka, (2011); Roderick, Nagaoka, Allensworth, Stoker, Correa, & Coca (2006); Roderick, Nagaoka, Coca, & Moeller (2008).

12 O'Connor (2009).

13 Allensworth et al. (2016a).

14 Mullins & Phillippe (2009).

15 College Board (2016a).

16 The percentage of undergraduates who received a Pell Grant went up from 24 percent in 2006-07 to 33 percent in 2015-16 (https://trends.collegeboard.org/student-aid/figures-tables/maximum-and-average-pell-grants-over-time). The maximum award of the Pell Grant went up from $4,055 in 2006-07 to $5,775 in 2015-06 in constant 2015 dollars, and the average

Pell Grant went up from $2,910 in 2006-07 to $3,724 in 2015-16 in constant 2015 dollars (https://trends.collegeboard.org/student-aid/figures-tables/maximum-and-average-pell-grants-over-time <Accessed March, 21,2017>); College Board (2016b).

17 Illinois Student Aid Commission (2012). The maximum award for FY 2013 covered about 51 percent of the cost at an Illinois community college.

18 The vast majority of CPS graduates qualify for free or reduced-price lunch (84 percent in 2015). For a discussion on the implications of college choices, see Fry (2009) and Mullin & Philippe (2009).

19 Dettro (2015, August 13); Geiger (2015, December 28); Woodhouse, K. (2016, January 7).

Meanwhile, the local community college landscape has seen a transformation that would suggest a growing interest in attending a two-year institution. Specifically, City Colleges has engaged in a concerted effort over the past five years to "reinvent" its system. Since 2010, they have restructured and revamped program offerings (e.g., College to Careers), updated their campus infrastructure, and provided the Chicago Star Scholarship for high-performing CPS graduates. Any of these changes over the last decade may have attracted recent CPS graduates who may not have otherwise considered City Colleges in the past, either because they did not consider college as a viable option or because they would have preferred to attend a four-year institution.

Finally, over the past decade, the city of Chicago has seen the emergence of non-profit organizations dedicated to easing the transition between high school and college.[20] These organizations go beyond traditional scholarship and tutoring programs and use a range of models. Some support individual CPS students through the college application and enrollment process, while others build the capacity of CPS school practitioners to support students. As high school budgets—and often the funds for college counselors—have dropped, these organizations have attempted to fill the gap and increase the number of students enrolling in college.

While we expect some of these changes in the education landscape to increase access to two-year and four-year college enrollment over this time period, others are likely to adversely affect college participation. Next, we report on descriptive patterns of CPS graduates' two-year and four-year enrollment in light of these contextual changes. Unless otherwise noted, all college enrollment data refer to the fall immediately following high school graduation.

College Enrollment Trends for CPS Graduates (2006-15)

A 2016 Consortium report on educational attainment indicated that CPS made significant gains in its rate of four-year enrollment over the last decade.[21] As we will show in the next section, recent rates of four-year enrollment among CPS graduates are in line with rates nationwide, and even surpass those of several other urban public school districts. In contrast, increases in two-year enrollment have been smaller, and recent rates of two-year enrollment among CPS graduates are below national rates and well below rates seen in other urban public school districts.

The rate of two-year enrollment for CPS graduates increased by 3 percentage points between 2006 and 2015 (**see Figure 1**). In more recent years, the trend for CPS rates of two-year enrollment has diverged from the four-year trend; while rates of four-year enrollment increased since 2013, the rates of two-year enrollment decreased slightly. This means that two-year enrollment now accounts for a smaller share of overall college enrollment than it has in the past (e.g., 33 percent of all enrollment in 2006 and 29 percent of all enrollment in 2015). This pattern confirms expectations of greater access to four-year institutions as a result of overall improvements in high school graduates' qualifications. At the same time, it challenges the notion that fewer financial supports over time would lead to decreased four-year enrollment.

Despite the recent drop in two-year enrollment rates, the number of CPS graduates attending two-year colleges actually grew by 1,165 students (a 45 percent increase in enrollment), because CPS now produces more graduates. In other words, while the proportion of CPS graduates who directly enrolled in a two-year college dropped slightly, more CPS graduates enrolled in a two-year college in 2015 than did a decade ago.

---

20 Examples of programs serving CPS students include Bottom Line, Chicago Scholars, College Possible, La Casa, Network for College Success, OneGoal, and Umoja Student Development Corporation.

21 Nagaoka & Healey (2016).

FIGURE 1

CPS Graduates' Immediate College Enrollment Rates Increased Over the Last Decade

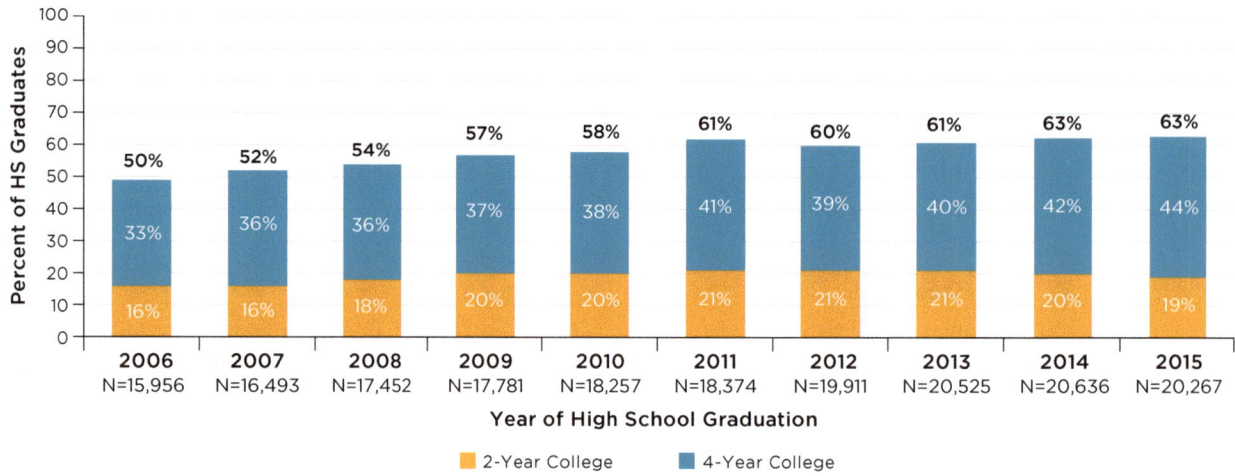

	2006	2007	2008	2009	2010	2011	2012	2013	2014	2015
Number of Total Immediate Enrollees										
2-Year	2,577	2,669	3,173	3,523	3,621	3,771	4,074	4,347	4,203	3,742
4-Year	5,311	5,893	6,279	6,547	7,003	7,515	7,844	8,251	8,755	8,988
Percent of Total Immediate Enrollees										
2-Year	33%	31%	34%	35%	34%	33%	34%	35%	32%	29%
4-Year	67%	69%	66%	65%	66%	67%	66%	65%	68%	71%

Note: Ns listed above refer to the number of high school graduates for each year. Percentages in stacked bars may not add up to numbers listed above stacked bars due to rounding. Data and methods are described in Appendix A.

Most CPS graduates who made an immediate transition to a two-year college attended a City College (**see Figure 2**). Moreover, the growth in two-year enrollment over the last decade has been largely at City Colleges. Interestingly, it appears that much of the growth in rates of immediate enrollment at City Colleges for CPS graduates occurred prior to City Colleges' recent reform efforts. It is possible, however, that City Colleges' reform efforts could have attracted students not captured in our analysis (e.g., high school graduates who delayed their enrollment; adults who entered college after spending an extended amount of time in the workplace).

What should we make of these local patterns of enrollment? The answer depends on whether we compare CPS rates to the nation as a whole, or to districts that more closely mirror the demographics of CPS graduates. The recent rates of overall college enrollment in CPS, for example, were below rates seen nationally (i.e. 63 percent in CPS vs. 69 percent nationally; **see Table 1**).[22] However, the population of Chicago Public Schools graduates was different, in numerous ways, from the population of all recent high school completers[23] in the United States. As shown in **Table 1**, the 2015 CPS rate of overall college enrollment (63 percent) was above the national rate among high school graduates who attended low-income[24] high schools (54 percent).[25]

The differences between CPS and the nation are more pronounced when we look at two-year enrollment and four-year enrollment separately. Compared to recent rates of two-year and four-year college enrollment in the United States, CPS had relatively low rates

---

22 McFarland et al. (2017).

23 National rates of college enrollment reported in Table 1 are of "recent high school completers," which include individuals ages 16 to 24 who graduated from high school or completed GED during the calendar year (McFarland et al., 2017).

24 Low-income schools are defined as schools where at least one-half of their students are eligible for free or reduced-price lunch (National Student Clearinghouse Research Center, 2016).

25 National Student Clearinghouse Research Center (2016).

FIGURE 2

Two-Year Enrollment Growth Was Mainly at City Colleges of Chicago

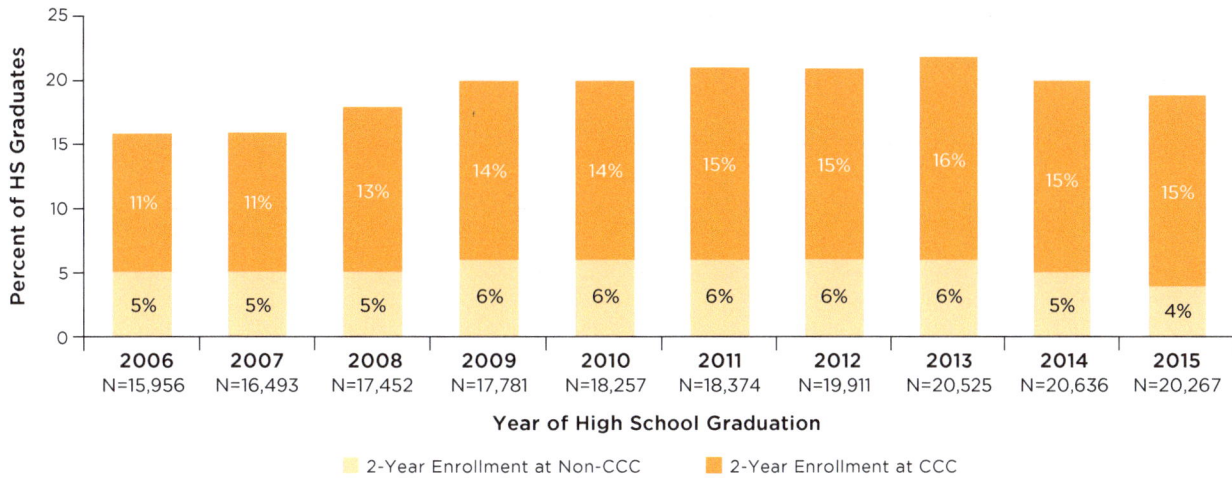

Note: Percentages in stacked bars may not add up to 2-year enrollment rates listed in Figure 1 due to rounding. Data and methods are described in Appendix A.

of two-year enrollment and relatively high rates of four-year enrollment. In fact, the CPS two-year enrollment rate was lower than rates of U.S. students who attended low-income high schools,[26] and also lower than rates of other urban school districts like Dallas,[27] Baltimore,[28] New York City,[29] and Los Angeles.[30] At the same time, Chicago's four-year enrollment rate (44 percent) significantly outpaced four-year college enrollment rates for U.S. students who attended low-income schools (29 percent), and rates of other urban districts, which ranged from 23 percent to 38 percent.

While CPS's enrollment trends are promising, a persistent challenge for public school districts is making sure that all students are exposed to educational opportunities that support college access. Gaps in college participation by race, gender, and income seen nationally suggest that such opportunities are uneven.[31] In the next chapter, we explore various gaps in college enrollment for CPS graduates.

TABLE 1

CPS Graduates Enrolled Directly in Two-Year Colleges at Lower Rates than Seen in Urban Districts and Nationally

District	Year	2-Year College Enrollment	4-Year College Enrollment	Total College Enrollment
Nation	**2015**	**25%**	**44%**	**69%**
New York	2012	27%	38%	65%
Chicago	**2015**	**19%**	**44%**	**63%**
Los Angeles	2015	37%	24%	61%
Nation: Low Income Schools	**2015**	**25%**	**29%**	**54%**
Dallas	2014	24%	25%	49%
Baltimore	2015	20%	23%	44%

Note: Percentages listed in "2-Year College Enrollment" and "4-Year College Enrollment" columns may not add up to the numbers listed in "Total College Enrollment" column due to rounding.

Sources: Nation: McFarland et al. (2017); **New York:** Coca (2014); **Los Angeles:** Jones (2016); **Nation, Low-Income Schools:** Kena et al. (2016); **Dallas:** Hall (2015); **Baltimore:** Durham, Ruiz, & Connolly (2017).

---

26 Kena et al. (2016).
27 Dallas Independent School District (2015).
28 Durham, Ruiz, & Connolly (2017).

29 Coca (2014).
30 Jones (2016).
31 DePaoli, Balfanz, & Bridgeland (2016).

Delayed College Enrollment Rates

An exploration of immediate transitions into college provides valuable information to CPS high schools, as this is a transition that teachers and counselors are well-positioned to influence. However, the focus on students' immediate transition masks the range of college enrollment experiences; many students enter college well after finishing high school. From a higher education perspective in particular, understanding patterns of enrollment means looking beyond immediate entry. For this reason, we briefly explore patterns of delayed enrollment for the class of 2009, which is the most recent cohort for which we can track first-time college enrollment within six years of graduating high school. By looking at delayed enrollment into college, we can better understand the full picture of college access—the flow into higher education over time, as well as the extent to which a graduating cohort will ultimately enroll in college.

While over half (57 percent) of the class of 2009 enrolled immediately in college—the fall following high school graduation—a significant share (19 percent) delayed college enrollment (see Figure A). This means that 76 percent of students—three out of four students—from the class of 2009 enrolled in college at some point within six years of finishing high school. Put differently, while most CPS graduates who matriculated into college did so immediately, a substantial minority delayed their entry. Delayed initial entry, however, differed greatly by level of college initially attended.

Among all 2009 CPS graduates, 37 percent made their initial enrollment in higher education at a four-year college in the fall immediately after high school. Only an additional five percent enrolled in a four-year college in the following five years—which means that almost nine out of ten students who started their college careers at a four-year college did so immediately after high school. Conversely, 20 percent of CPS graduates made their initial enrollment in higher education at a two-year college immediately after high school. An additional 14 percent of graduates made their first entry into higher education at a two-year college in the following five years—which means that 42 percent of all students who started their college careers at a two-year college delayed entry. This pattern of delayed entry into two-year colleges suggests these schools offer a more flexible post-secondary option.[A] However, this flexibility often comes at a cost; research has shown that students who delay college entry are less likely to attain a college degree than those who enter college directly after high school, even after controlling for measurable differences across the two groups.[B]

As we broaden the scope of our future work in ways that also speak to the interests of those in higher education, we will include a wider array of students in our subsequent analyses. This is important because students who take "non-traditional" paths into and through higher education, like those who delay enrollment, make up an important population that post-secondary institutions serve.

FIGURE A

19 Percent of 2009 CPS Graduates Delayed Enrolling in College

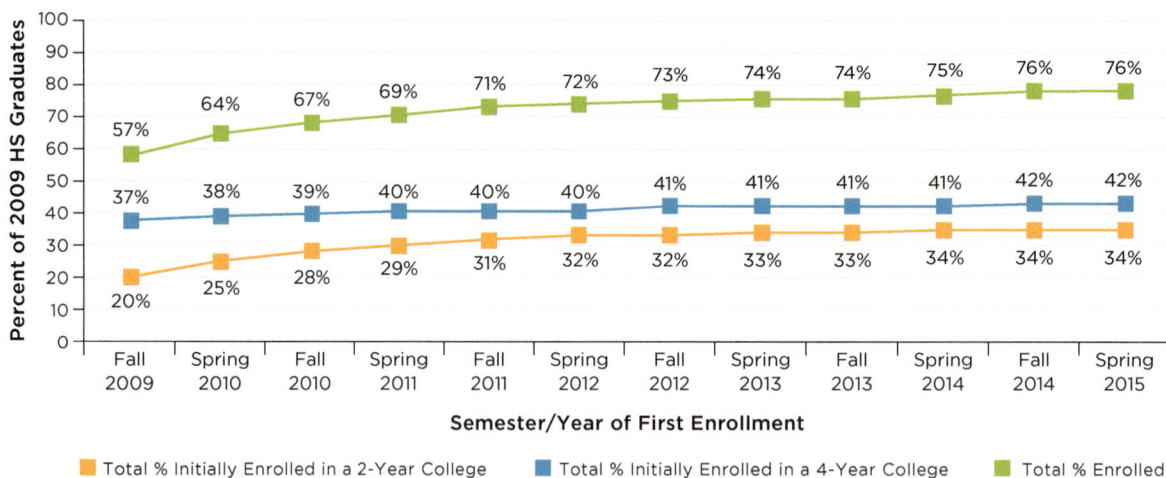

Note: Percentages of 2-year and 4-year enrollees may not add up to total enrollees due to rounding. Data and methods are described in Appendix A.

A   Horn, Cataldi, & Sikora (2005).

B   Berkner, He, & Cataldi (2002); Horn et al. (2005); Bozick & DeLuca (2005); Turner (2004).

CHAPTER 2

Patterns of Enrollment by Student and School Characteristics

In this chapter, we report rates of college enrollment for the class of 2015, the most recent cohort of CPS graduates for which we have data, disaggregated across different characteristics. We look at patterns of college enrollment by student demographic characteristics (race/ethnicity, gender, and socioeconomic background), by academic characteristics (grades and test scores), and by school characteristics (selective enrollment, charter, and other CPS high schools). To place these disaggregated college enrollment rates into a broader context, we first report on national rates of college enrollment by comparable student subgroups. In several cases, gaps between the college enrollment rates of student subgroups in Chicago line up with gaps seen across the United States.

Current College Enrollment Patterns in the United States

National studies have consistently shown sizable gaps in college enrollment rates by student background characteristics like racial/ethnic group,[32] gender,[33] and family income.[34] For instance, prior studies have found that Black and Latino high school graduates are less likely than their White and Asian counterparts to enroll in college immediately after finishing high school; and when Black and Latino students do attend college, they are also more likely to enroll in a two-year college than a four-year institution. Studies on college enrollment patterns by gender find that female high school graduates enroll in college at higher rates than their male counterparts—a pattern that started in the late 1980s.[35] Studies using national datasets have also shown low-income students are less likely to enroll in college than their high-income counterparts; moreover,

low-income students are severely under-represented in selective post-secondary institutions.[36] Recent national statistics suggest that these gaps are enduring.

Nationally, as shown in **Table 2**, Black and Latino high school graduates had lower rates of overall college enrollment (63 percent and 67 percent, respectively) in comparison to their White and Asian counterparts (70 percent and 87 percent, respectively)—a gap of approximately 7 percentage points between White and Black students and 2 percentage points between White and Latino students.[37] Rates of overall college enrollment among female high school graduates surpassed those of male high school graduates by almost 7 percentage points (73 percent versus 66 percent).[38] Low-income high school graduates were as likely to enroll in college as middle-

TABLE 2

National Rates of College Enrollment Disaggregated by Subgroup

	Percent of 2014 High School Graduates Enrolled in 2-Year and 4-Year Colleges*
White	70
Black	63
Latino	67
Asian	87
Male	66
Female	73
Low Income	63
Middle Income	63
High Income	83

* Three-year moving averages are reported for college enrollment rates by race/ethnicity and level of family income.

Source: McFarland et al. (2017).

---

32 DePaoli et al. (2016); Fry (2011); Karen (2002); Reardon, Baker, & Klasik (2012).
33 Bailey & Dynarski (2011); DiPrete & Buchmann (2014); Goldin, Katz, & Kuziemko (2006).
34 Bailey & Dynarski (2011); Hearn (1991); Reardon et al. (2012).
35 Buchmann, DiPrete, & McDaniel (2008); Cho (2007); Goldin et al. (2006).
36 Bailey & Dynarski (2011); Hearn (1991); Reardon et al. (2012).
37 NCES numbers reported are from the three-year moving average in 2015 (McFarland et al., 2017).
38 McFarland et al. (2017).

income students (63 percent)—but high-income graduates' enrollment rates were 20 percentage points higher than their low-income and middle-income counterparts.[39]

Current College Enrollment Patterns in Chicago

By Race/Ethnicity and Gender

The gaps in rates of immediate enrollment by race/ethnicity were much wider in Chicago than gaps seen nationally. Specifically, Black and Latino graduates from the class of 2015 had rates of overall college enrollment that ranged from 15 to 25 percentage points lower than their respective White and Asian counterparts (**see Figure 3**).[40] The size of the gap in Chicago, however, appears to be largely driven by disproportionately high rates of enrollment for White CPS graduates (80 percent for females, and 73 percent for males) in comparison to rates for White high school completers across the country (70 percent). This discrepancy in rates of college enrollment suggests that

White high school graduates in Chicago, who accounted for less than 10 percent of all CPS graduates in 2015, differ from the overall population of White high school completers in the United States, although it is unclear which characteristics contribute to that difference.

The differences in CPS graduates' enrollment rates by race/ethnicity were primarily driven by four-year college enrollment rates. Latino graduates had the lowest rates of four-year college enrollment in comparison to the rates of other racial/ethnic groups in their respective gender group. Black graduates also enrolled in a four-year college at lower rates than their respective Asian or White counterparts. In terms of two-year enrollment, more Latino graduates attended a two-year college in comparison to Black, White, and Asian graduates; this finding is consistent with the prior research.[41] We should note that college enrollment rates in this report likely represent an undercount of undocumented students, although the extent of its impact on different racial/ethnic groups is unclear.[42]

FIGURE 3

Latino Graduates Had the Lowest Rates of Overall College Enrollment, and the Highest Share of Two-Year Enrollment

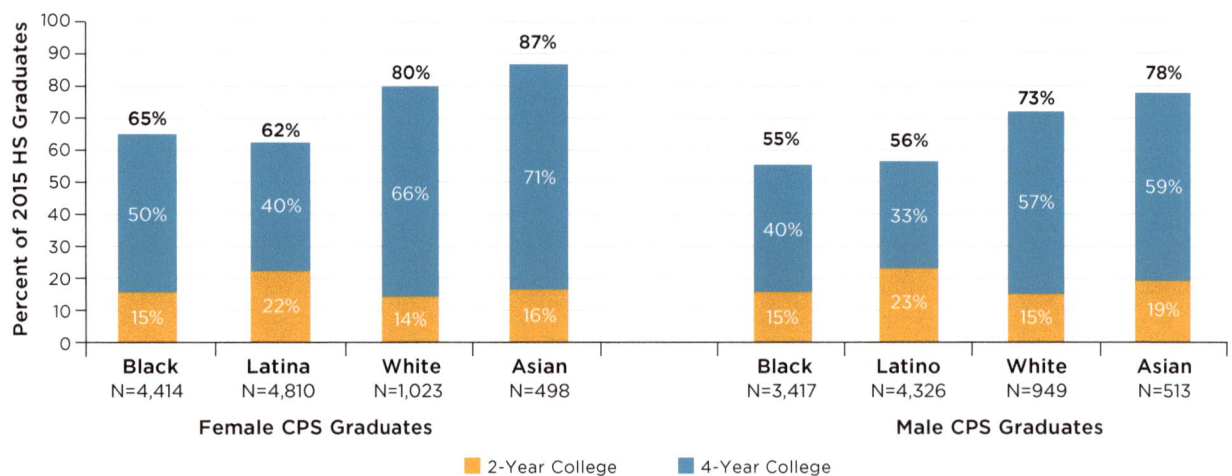

Note: Ns listed above refer to the number of 2015 high school graduates in each group. Ns and percentages do not include Native American students, Alaskan Native students, multiracial students or students with missing racial/ethnic information (317 students in 2015). Percentages in stacked bars may not add up to numbers listed above stacked bars due to rounding. Data and methods are described in Appendix A.

39 NCES numbers reported are from the three-year moving average in 2015 (McFarland et al., 2017).

40 In the UChicago Consortium 2006 publication, *From high school to the future: A first look at Chicago public school graduates' college enrollment, college preparation, and graduation from four-year colleges*, we reported similar gaps in overall rates of college participation in 2002 and 2003 by race/ethnicity and gender (Roderick et al., 2006).

The UChicago Consortium 2014 update provided four-year college enrollment rates by race/ethnicity and gender, but did not show rates for two-year colleges (Healey, Nagaoka, & Michelman, 2014).

41 Adelman (2005); Hurwitz & Kumar (2015).

42 The National Student Clearinghouse estimates that less than 50 percent of undocumented four-year college enrollees are accounted for in the data they receive.

As shown in **Figure 3**, Chicago had similar gaps in overall college enrollment rates by gender to those seen nationwide (**shown in Table 2 on p.9**). Gaps in rates of overall enrollment were the result of differences in rates of four-year enrollment; enrollment at two-year colleges was not dramatically different by gender. When also considering race /ethnicity, the gender gap was most pronounced for Black high school graduates (a 10 percentage point difference), and least pronounced for Latino graduates (a 6 percentage point difference).

By Socioeconomic Background

We cannot directly compare national statistics on college enrollment to those of CPS graduates using the same categories of family income, because we do not have family income information for CPS students. However, we can explore differences in college enrollment patterns by income using the median family income of a student's census block as a proxy for CPS students' socioeconomic background.[43]

Overall, CPS graduates who lived in census blocks with high[44] median family income enrolled in college at higher rates than CPS graduates from census blocks with low median family income, as **Figure 4** shows. Moreover, the differences in college enrollment between these two groups appeared to be largely driven by differential rates of four-year enrollment: The share of CPS graduates from low median family income census blocks who enrolled in a four-year college was 16 percentage points lower than their peers from high median family income census blocks (39 percent vs. 55 percent, respectively), while two-year enrollment rates were nearly the same (18 percent vs. 17 percent, respectively).

Although smaller than gaps by family income seen nationally, the gaps in overall enrollment for CPS graduates underscore the enduring and widespread impact

FIGURE 4

Four-Year College Enrollment Rates Differed More by Socioeconomic Background than Two-Year College Enrollment Rates

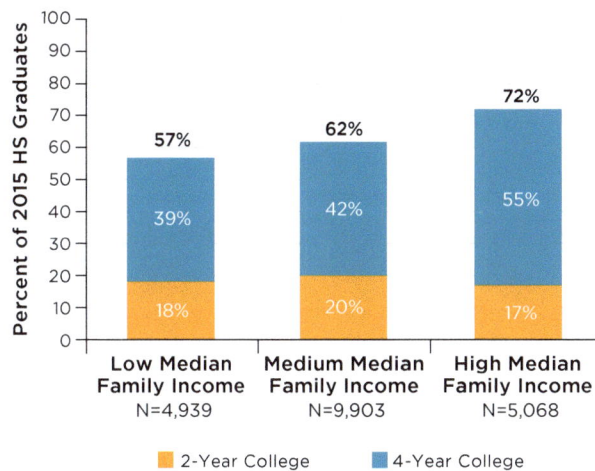

Note: Ns listed above refer to the number of 2015 high school graduates in each group. Ns and percentages do not include students residing in areas with missing Census information (357 students in 2015). The median family income of a student's census block is used as a proxy for students' socioeconomic backgrounds. The category "High median family income" includes census blocks that have a median family income at or above $61,538. The category "Medium median family income" includes census blocks that have a median family income that is above $32,917 and below $61,538. The category "Low median family income" includes census blocks that have a median family income at or below $32,917. Data and methods are described in Appendix A.

that socioeconomic background has on students' access to a post-secondary institution. Higher socioeconomic status is associated with greater access to financial resources to pay for college (e.g., financial capital) as well as wider access to social networks and resources to support college planning (e.g., social capital). While these gaps in college enrollment are troubling, prior research finds that these differences are largely explained—and in some cases are reversed—when accounting for differences in students' academic qualifications, such as grades and exam scores.[45] This suggests a complicated interplay among academic preparation, college costs, and socioeconomic status in students' college options and enrollment patterns.

---

43 Information on the median family income of a student's census block comes from the Census' American Community Survey data that has been linked, at the census block-group level, with students' residential information. A student's own family income may be higher or lower than the value of her census block's median family income. Thus, by using this proxy we expect the size of the enrollment gap to be an underestimate—though we do not expect vastly different results than if we had income data for each family.

44 The category "High median family income" includes census blocks that have a median family income at or above $61,538. The category "Medium median family income" includes census blocks that have a median family income that is above $32,917 and below $61,538. The category "Low median family income" includes census blocks that have a median family income at or below $32,917.

45 Buchmann et al. (2008); Kurlaender (2006); Perna (2000).

By Graduating GPAs

Academic qualifications, particularly grades, play a central role in college admission decisions. In 2015, GPAs—for those who have reported grades[46]—continued to be a good predictor of college enrollment of CPS graduates. **Figure 5** shows that high school graduates with very low GPAs were unlikely to enroll in any college; when they did attend college, they were more likely to attend a two-year college than a four-year college. Not surprisingly, CPS graduates needed at least a 2.5 GPA to have had close to a 50 percent likelihood of enrolling in a four-year college. This suggests that grades are an important lever with which to increase access to college, and are particularly important to gain access to four-year colleges. Unfortunately, we do not have a national comparison group for college enrollment by GPA. It is also important to note that—unlike enrollment by ACT scores (**Figure 6**)—**Figure 5** does not include charter school students, who constituted 17 percent of 2015 graduates. We do not know what effect the inclusion of this important population on enrollment rates by GPA would be.

By ACT Scores

Like grades, scores on college entrance exams like the SAT and ACT also play an important role in college admission and, in turn, patterns of enrollment.[47] While 20 percent of CPS graduates had missing GPA information, all CPS students were required to take the ACT exam as a part of the state accountability system; therefore, our data on ACT scores are more comprehensive (only 3 percent missing). In 2015, CPS graduates with higher ACT scores had higher overall rates of college participation and higher rates of four-year enrollment than those with lower ACT scores (**see Figure 6**). In fact, CPS graduates needed at least an 18 on the ACT to have had at least a 50 percent probability of enrolling in a four-year college. Thus, improvements to student performance on college entrance exams appear to be another potential lever for increasing college access.

By Type of High School

While it is apparent that academic achievement is associated with college enrollment patterns, other studies

FIGURE 5

Students with Lower Grades Had Lower Overall College Enrollment Rates and Higher Rates of Two-Year Enrollment

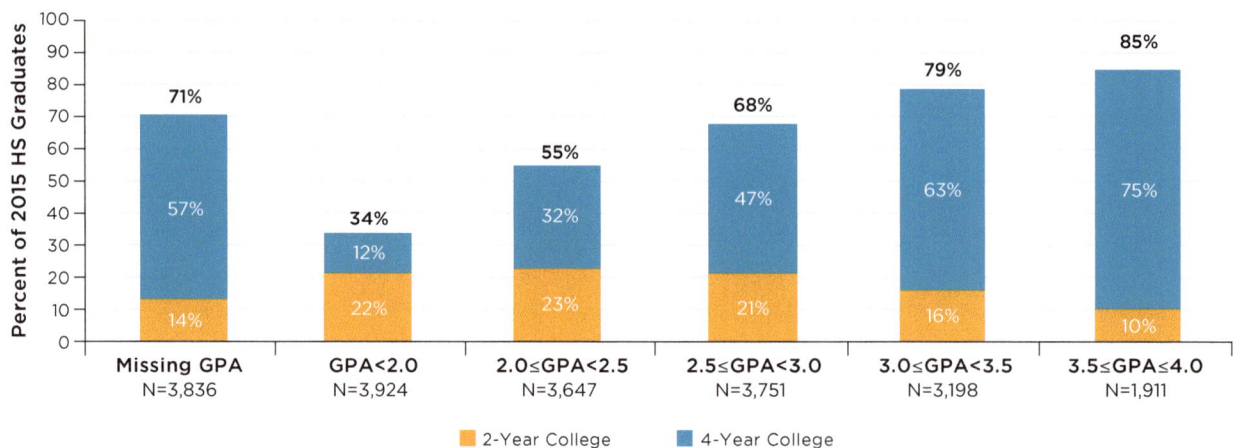

Note: Ns listed above refer to the number of 2015 high school graduates in each group. Percentages in stacked bars may not add up to numbers listed above stacked bars due to rounding. Data and methods are described in Appendix A.

[46] About 20 percent of CPS high school graduates in 2015 have missing GPA information. The vast majority of these students (93 percent) attended charter high schools. Many CPS charter schools use different student information systems from the IMPACT system used by non-charter schools. Because each system varies in the way that it stores information about courses, credits, teachers, periods, grades, and other data, creating linkages across systems is a difficult, and our data

archive currently does not include records of charter school students' course performance. We are therefore unable to include charter school students in GPA analyses. Figures using GPA (Figures 5, 8, and 10) do not include students with missing GPA information, who are mainly from charter schools. GPAs that we use are cumulative, unweighted GPA.

[47] Roderick et al. (2006).

FIGURE 6

Students with Lower ACT Scores Had Lower Overall College Enrollment Rates but Higher Rates of Two-Year Enrollment

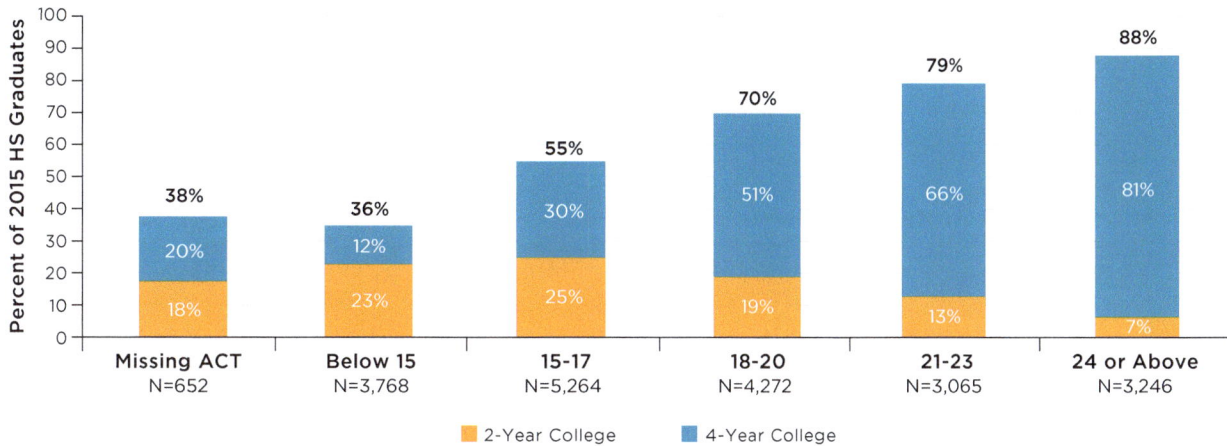

Note: Ns listed above refer to the number of 2015 high school graduates in each group. Percentages in stacked bars may not add up to numbers listed above stacked bars due to rounding. Data and methods are described in Appendix A.

suggest that high schools could also shape students' post-secondary choices beyond the academic preparation they provide.[48] In this section, we briefly explore the type of CPS high school attended as another potential source of variation in students' college outcomes.

Previous Consortium research has indicated that high school graduation rates and rates of four-year college enrollment differed widely by type of high school attended.[49] Here, we expand on these findings by examining whether differences in high school graduation rates and four-year enrollment rates also translate into differences in two-year enrollment and, in turn, overall rates of college enrollment.

For the class of 2015, patterns of two-year college enrollment and overall college enrollment vary by the type of high school attended (**see Figure 7**). For instance, graduates of selective enrollment high schools (15 percent of CPS graduates) had the highest rates of overall college enrollment, in comparison to rates of graduates of charter high schools (18 percent of CPS graduates) and graduates of all other CPS high

schools[50] (68 percent of CPS graduates). Moreover, much of the difference between selective enrollment high schools and other high schools is due to differential rates of four-year enrollment. Given that selective enrollment high schools only admit high-achieving students and serve relatively smaller shares of students who qualify for free or reduced-price lunch, it comes as no surprise that graduates of these high schools outpace graduates at other CPS high schools in terms of their college participation.[51] Notably, a recent study of CPS selective enrollment students found that other high-achieving students in the district who did not enroll in selective enrollment schools—because they just missed the cutoff needed to attend these schools—had similar on-time high school graduation rates and overall college participation rates.[52]

Charter school graduates had a similar rate of overall college enrollment (71 percent) compared to graduates of other CPS high schools with high student achievement (71 percent), and a much higher rate than graduates of other neighborhood high schools with medium

48 McDonough (1997).

49 Gwynne & Moore (forthcoming); Nagaoka & Healey (2016).

50 This category of high schools includes a wide variety of high schools (e.g., career academies, military academies, magnet, other non-charter neighborhood high schools) and accounts for the majority of CPS graduates.

51 Barrow, Sartain, & de la Torre (2016); Allensworth, Moore, Sartain, & de la Torre (2016b).

52 Barrow et al. (2016).

FIGURE 7

Students in High Schools with Low ACT Scores Had Lower Overall Rates of College-Going but Higher Rates of Two-Year Enrollment

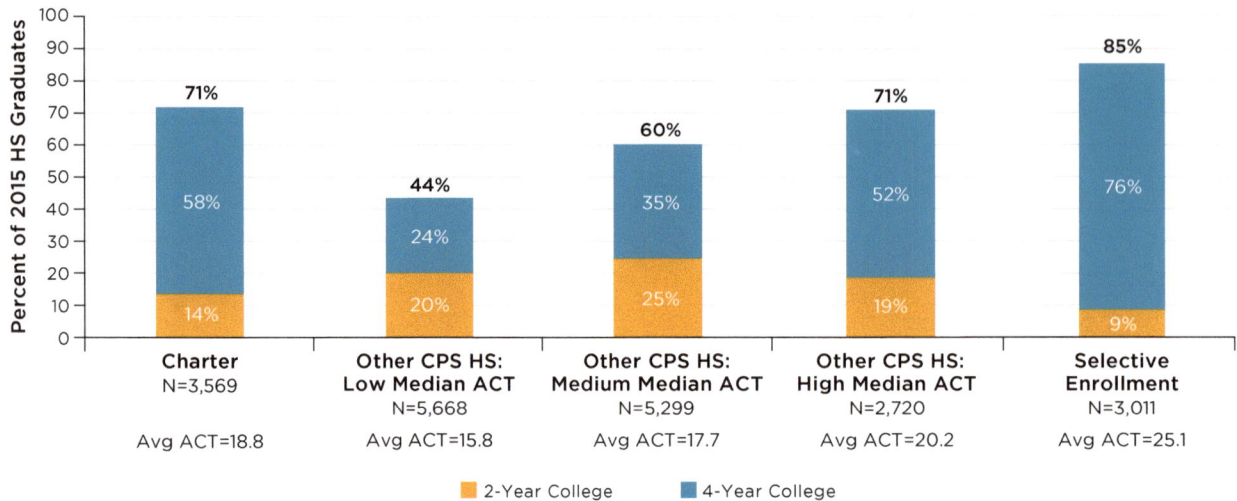

Note: Ns listed above refer to the number of 2015 high school graduates in each group. Percentages in stacked bars may not add up to numbers listed above stacked bars due to rounding. Data and methods are described in Appendix A. The category "Low Median ACT" includes schools with a median ACT score at 16 or below. The category of "Medium Median ACT" includes schools with a median ACT score above 16, but below 19. The category "High Median ACT" includes schools with a median ACT score at 19 or above.

and low levels of student achievement (60 percent and 44 percent, respectively). Charter school graduates had a slightly higher rate of four-year enrollment than that graduates of other, non-selective enrollment CPS high schools with high student achievement (58 percent versus 52 percent). A forthcoming Consortium study of charter schools finds that, using a matched comparison group, students in charter schools were more likely to enroll in a four-year college than similar students enrolled elsewhere.[53] However, more research is needed to understand why these students have different enrollment rates.

It is worth noting that the student and school characteristics discussed in this section are interconnected. For example, Black and Latino students in Chicago are less likely to live in an advantaged neighborhood than their White and Asian counterparts,[54] and students living in an advantaged neighborhood are more likely to attend selective enrollment high schools.[55] In turn, the college enrollment patterns reported by one subgroup could reflect multiple factors rather than just one. A more sophisticated analysis is needed in order to detect the unique effect of any one of the attributes examined in this report.

Altogether, these descriptive patterns of enrollment raise several questions about who attends college, who attends four-year colleges, and who does not enroll college in the fall after high school graduation. For instance, do students enroll at a level of college (e.g., two-year or four-year) consistent with their eligibility to attend, given their academic credentials? Prior research by the UChicago Consortium and others has shown that a sizeable share of high school graduates have enrolled in colleges to which they are academically overqualified to attend, or have not immediately enrolled in college.[56] In the next section, we ask: Once CPS graduates sort themselves among their college choices, do four-year colleges serve CPS graduates with different academic characteristics (e.g., grades and ACT scores) than two-year institutions? Do the academic characteristics of CPS graduates who attend community colleges look similar to the academic characteristics of CPS graduates who do not enroll in college after finishing high school?

53 Gwynne & Moore (forthcoming).

54 Among 2015 CPS graduates, only 18 percent of Black students and 22 percent of Latino students lived in a high-median income neighborhood, whereas 66 percent of White students and 36 percent of Asian students did.

55 Among 2015 CPS graduates, 8 percent of students who lived in a neighborhood with low-median family income attended a selective enrollment high school, whereas 23 percent of students from high-median family income families did.

56 Roderick et al. (2006); Roderick et al. (2011); Roderick, Nagaoka, Coca, & Moeller (2009); Smith, Pender, Howell, & Hurwitz (2012); Bowen, Chingos, & McPherson (2009).

CHAPTER 3

Academic Characteristics of Students by Enrollment Status

Yet another lens through which to investigate patterns of college enrollment is from the post-secondary perspective. Specifically, it is useful to know more about the CPS graduates who attend various post-secondary institutions or types of institutions, particularly given a growing interest in comparing post-secondary outcomes across the selectivity institutions or across specific institutions. This chapter investigates the pre-college academic profiles of recent CPS graduates by their enrollment status immediately after high school—those who did not immediately enroll in college, those who immediately enrolled in a two-year college, and those who immediately enrolled in a four-year college. In addition, we report pre-college academic profiles of recent CPS graduates by the most commonly attended local post-secondary institutions.

First, we provide additional context with which to decipher enrollment patterns in Chicago by reporting pre-college academic profiles by enrollment status for a recent set of U.S. high school graduates.[57] Nationally, about 90 percent of 2013 high school graduates who enrolled in a four-year college had at least a 2.5 GPA, compared to only 62 percent of two-year enrollees and 45 percent of non-enrollees (**see Table 3**). In other words, enrollees at four-year colleges tended to have stronger academic qualifications than enrollees at two-year colleges and those who do not enroll in college. However, the flipside of this result means that a notable group of high school graduates who did not enroll in college or who enrolled in a two-year college had GPAs that would presumably give them access to a four-year institution. This pattern supports a wide array of studies that suggests non-academic factors, such as economic factors, social resources, and financial resources, also influence student post-secondary decisions. There is little reason to believe that the patterns of enrollment seen nationwide are dramatically different from those found in Chicago.

TABLE 3

Nationally, 91 Percent Four-Year Enrollees Had At Least a 2.5 High School GPA

	GPA Below 2.0	2.0≤GPA<2.5	2.5≤GPA<3.0	3.0≤GPA<3.5	GPA 3.5 or Higher
All HS Diploma Holders	13%	18%	22%	22%	26%
Did Not Enroll	29%	27%	24%	14%	7%
Enrolled in 2-Year College	14%	25%	28%	21%	13%
Enrolled in 4-Year College	2%	7%	18%	27%	46%

Note: Percentages in rows may not add up to 100 due to rounding.

Source: Numbers are for the 2013 high school graduates and were calculated using National Center for Education Statistics' QuickStats for the High School Longitudinal Study of 2009.

[57] Numbers were calculated using National Center for Education Statistics' QuickStats for the High School Longitudinal Study of 2009.

By Immediate Enrollment Status

Among CPS 2015 graduates for whom we have GPAs,[58] a little over three-quarters who enrolled directly in a four-year college had at least a 2.5 GPA, while the GPAs of two-year enrollees and non-enrollees were much lower in comparison (see Figure 8). Interestingly, CPS non-enrollees and two-year college enrollees were more likely to have GPAs below 2.5 than their counterparts nationally. Both two-year and non-enrollees included relatively large groups of students with GPAs below 2.5 (54 percent and 67 percent, respectively), but CPS graduates who did not immediately enroll in college had the lowest GPAs (41 percent had GPAs below 2.0).

When examining students' ACT scores by enrollment status, results line up with findings on GPA profiles; higher achievement leads to higher enrollment rates. Namely, CPS graduates who enrolled in four-year colleges immediately after high school had much higher ACT composite scores than their counterparts who

enrolled in two-year colleges and those who did not immediately enroll in college. In fact, more than half of CPS four-year enrollees had an ACT composite score of at least 21 (53 percent), whereas only 17 percent of two-year enrollees and 15 percent of non-enrollees did (see Figure 9). Like grades, though, the differences in ACT scores between non-enrollees and two-year enrollees were small with the exception of a higher share of non-enrollees with ACT scores below 15.[59] This suggests that something other than ACT and GPA is driving students' decisions to immediately enroll in a two-year college or not enroll at all.

This descriptive look at academic profiles by enrollment status demonstrates that enrollment patterns are closely aligned to students' level of academic preparation. Yet it also reveals that many students do not enroll despite being academically prepared, and that many do enroll in college despite their relatively low levels of academic preparation. The patterns

FIGURE 8

Almost Half of CPS Two-Year Enrollees Had at Least a 2.5 High School GPA

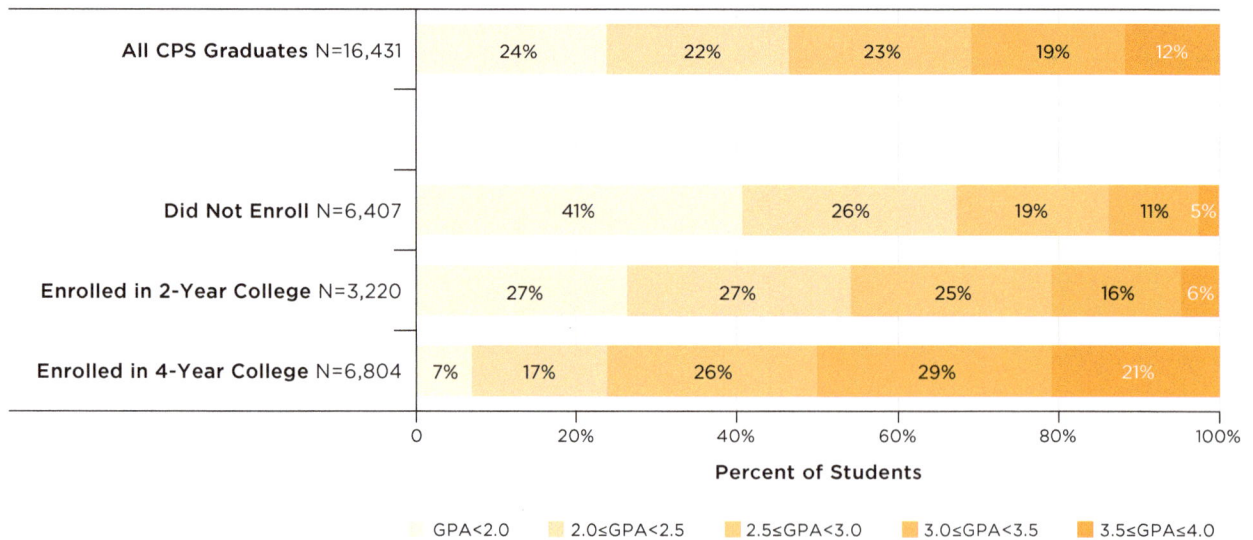

Percent of Students

Legend: GPA<2.0 | 2.0≤GPA<2.5 | 2.5≤GPA<3.0 | 3.0≤GPA<3.5 | 3.5≤GPA≤4.0

Note: Ns listed above refer to the number of 2015 high school graduates in each group. Ns and percentages do not include students missing GPA information (3,836 students). Percentages may not add up to 100 due to rounding. Data and methods are described in Appendix A.

---

58 About 20 percent of CPS high school graduates in 2015 have missing GPA information. The vast majority of these students (93 percent) attended charter high schools. Many CPS charter schools use different student information systems from the IMPACT system used by non-charter schools. Because each system varies in the way that it stores information about courses, credits, teachers, periods, grades, and other data, creating linkages across systems is a difficult, and our data

archive currently does not include records of charter school students' course performance. We are therefore unable to include charter school students in GPA analyses. Figures using GPA (Figures 5, 8, and 10) do not include students with missing GPA information, who are mainly from charter schools. GPAs that we use are cumulative, unweighted GPA.

59 ACT, Inc. (2015).

reported here also suggest that students' decisions to attend college and to attend a four-year institution are likely based on a number of factors, some of which are not related to academic background (e.g., family obligations, financial burdens, geographic preferences); a greater understanding of the college search and application process is needed to identify and address these additional factors.

By Institution Attended

Looking at two-year or four-year college enrollees in the aggregate hides the considerable variation of incoming students' achievement within and across two-year and four-year institutions. To examine variation in GPA[60] and ACT profiles by institution, we examined the incoming CPS student profiles among the 20 most commonly attended local post-secondary institutions attended by the class of 2015. We also included two very selective local universities, the University of Chicago

and Northwestern University; these very selective institutions provide a stark counterpoint to results listed for the 20 most commonly attended institutions. The institutions in **Figures 10 and 11** are grouped by sector (two-year vs. four-year institutions); and, for four-year colleges, by selectivity (non-selective, somewhat selective, selective, and very selective).[61]

The differences in GPA and ACT profiles of CPS graduates across four-year institutions were larger than across two-year institutions, as **Figures 10 and 11** show. This pattern is not surprising, given the variation in admission standards used at four-year institutions and the open admission policies across two-year institutions. Still, some four-year institutions (e.g., Northeastern Illinois University and Southern Illinois University) appeared to serve CPS graduates with academic credentials that were similar to those at some two-year colleges (e.g., such City Colleges as Richard J. Daley and Harold Washington). This pattern suggests

FIGURE 9

About 40 Percent of CPS Two-Year Enrollees Had at Least an 18 on the ACT

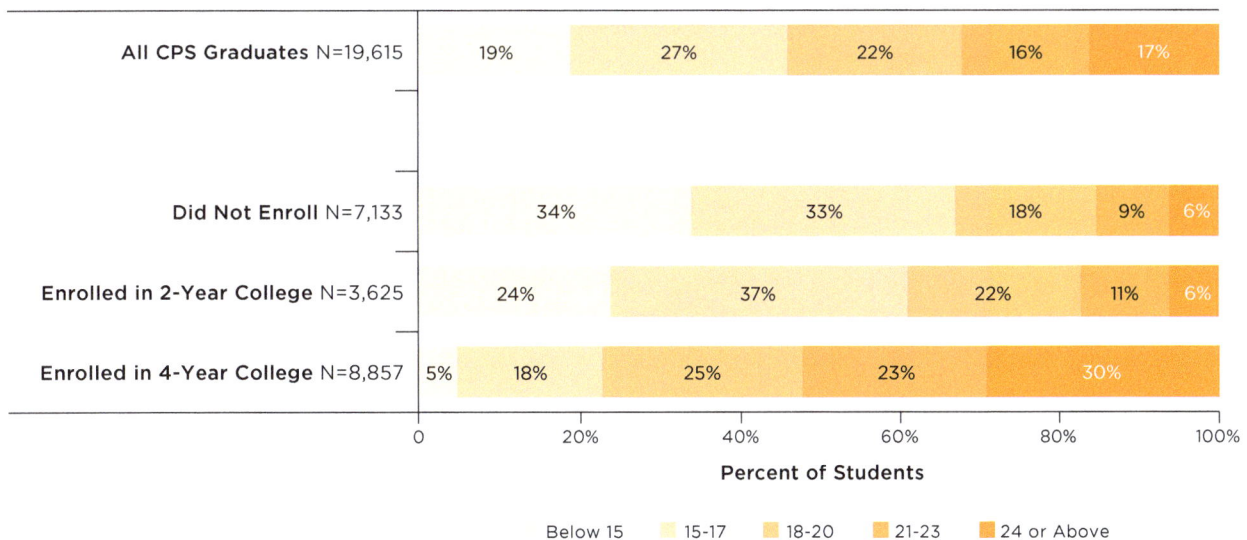

	Below 15	15-17	18-20	21-23	24 or Above
All CPS Graduates N=19,615	19%	27%	22%	16%	17%
Did Not Enroll N=7,133	34%	33%	18%	9%	6%
Enrolled in 2-Year College N=3,625	24%	37%	22%	11%	6%
Enrolled in 4-Year College N=8,857	5%	18%	25%	23%	30%

Percent of Students

Note: Ns listed above refer to the number of 2015 high school graduates in each group. Ns and percentages do not include students missing ACT scores (652 students). Percentages may not add up to 100 due to rounding. Data and methods are described in Appendix A.

60 About 20 percent of CPS high school graduates in 2015 have missing GPA information. The vast majority of these students (93 percent) attended charter high schools. Many CPS charter schools use different student information systems from the IMPACT system used by non-charter schools. Because each system varies in the way that it stores information about courses, credits, teachers, periods, grades, and other data, creating linkages across systems is a difficult, and our data archive currently does not include records of charter school

students' course performance. We are therefore unable to include charter school students in GPA analyses. Figures using GPA (Figures 5, 8, and 10) do not include students with missing GPA information, who are mainly from charter schools. GPAs that we use are cumulative, unweighted GPA.

61 Selectivity categories are based on Barron's competitiveness categories. We collapse the top two Barron's categories into the "very selective" category and the bottom two categories into the "nonselective" category (Barron's College Division, 2016).

that even students with moderately low academic qualifications have access to a four-year college. At the same time, this pattern raises questions about where students with moderately low academic qualifications will fare better, in terms of their likelihood of attaining a post-secondary degree, as well as their job and earnings prospects afterwards.

FIGURE 10

There Was Considerable Variability in Students' High School GPAs by Institutions Attended

2-Year Colleges

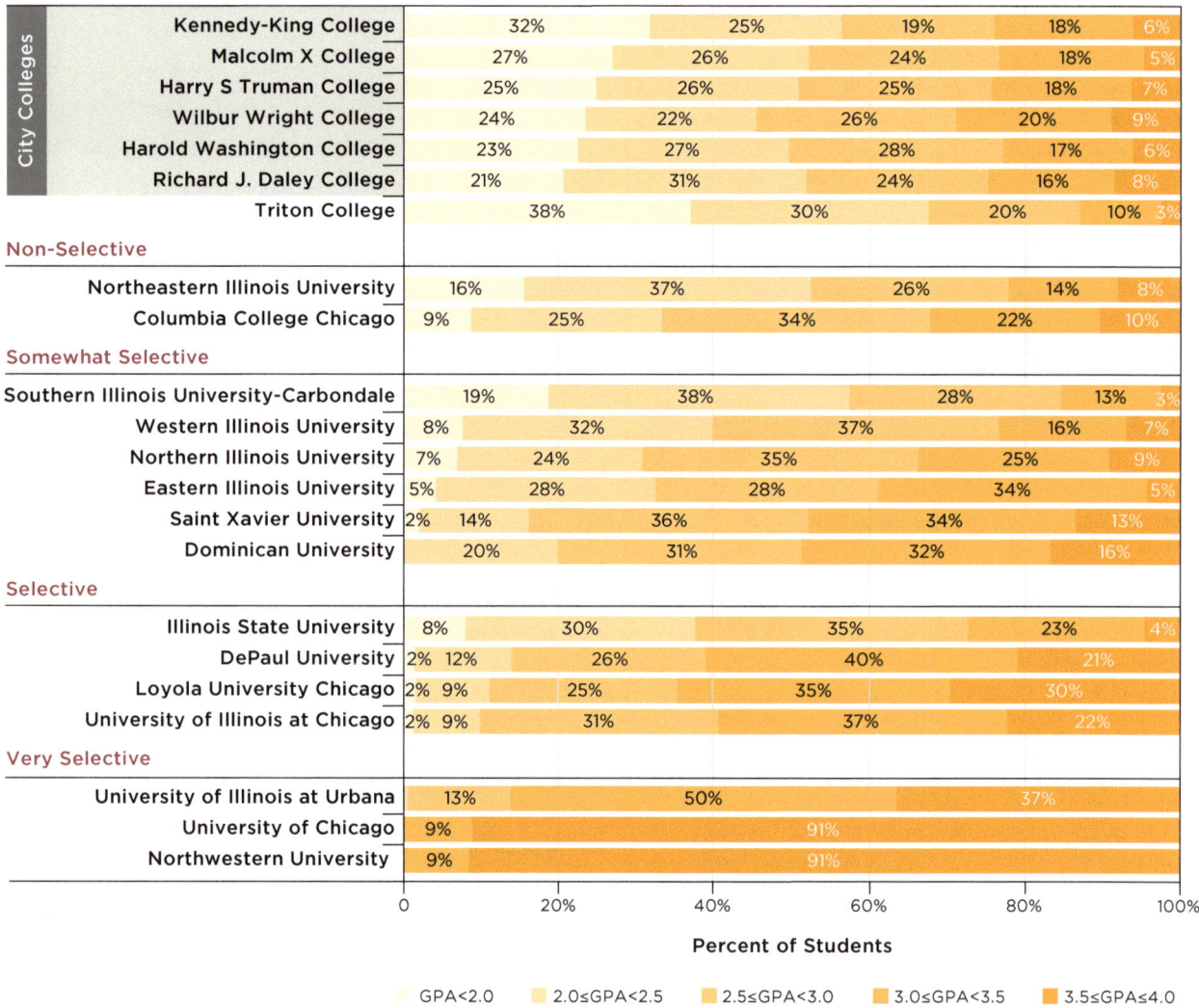

City Colleges	GPA<2.0	2.0≤GPA<2.5	2.5≤GPA<3.0	3.0≤GPA<3.5	3.5≤GPA≤4.0
Kennedy-King College	32%	25%	19%	18%	6%
Malcolm X College	27%	26%	24%	18%	5%
Harry S Truman College	25%	26%	25%	18%	7%
Wilbur Wright College	24%	22%	26%	20%	9%
Harold Washington College	23%	27%	28%	17%	6%
Richard J. Daley College	21%	31%	24%	16%	8%
Triton College	38%	30%	20%	10%	3%

Non-Selective

	GPA<2.0	2.0≤GPA<2.5	2.5≤GPA<3.0	3.0≤GPA<3.5	3.5≤GPA≤4.0
Northeastern Illinois University	16%	37%	26%	14%	8%
Columbia College Chicago	9%	25%	34%	22%	10%

Somewhat Selective

	GPA<2.0	2.0≤GPA<2.5	2.5≤GPA<3.0	3.0≤GPA<3.5	3.5≤GPA≤4.0
Southern Illinois University-Carbondale	19%	38%	28%	13%	3%
Western Illinois University	8%	32%	37%	16%	7%
Northern Illinois University	7%	24%	35%	25%	9%
Eastern Illinois University	5%	28%	28%	34%	5%
Saint Xavier University	2%	14%	36%	34%	13%
Dominican University		20%	31%	32%	16%

Selective

	GPA<2.0	2.0≤GPA<2.5	2.5≤GPA<3.0	3.0≤GPA<3.5	3.5≤GPA≤4.0
Illinois State University	8%	30%	35%	23%	4%
DePaul University	2%	12%	26%	40%	21%
Loyola University Chicago	2%	9%	25%	35%	30%
University of Illinois at Chicago	2%	9%	31%	37%	22%

Very Selective

	GPA<2.0	2.0≤GPA<2.5	2.5≤GPA<3.0	3.0≤GPA<3.5	3.5≤GPA≤4.0
University of Illinois at Urbana			13%	50%	37%
University of Chicago				9%	91%
Northwestern University				9%	91%

Percent of Students

Legend: GPA<2.0 | 2.0≤GPA<2.5 | 2.5≤GPA<3.0 | 3.0≤GPA<3.5 | 3.5≤GPA≤4.0

Note: Percentages do not include students missing GPA information. Percentages may not add up to 100 due to rounding. Data and methods are described in Appendix A.

FIGURE 11

Students Enrolled in the Same Colleges Had Very Different ACT Scores

2-Year Colleges

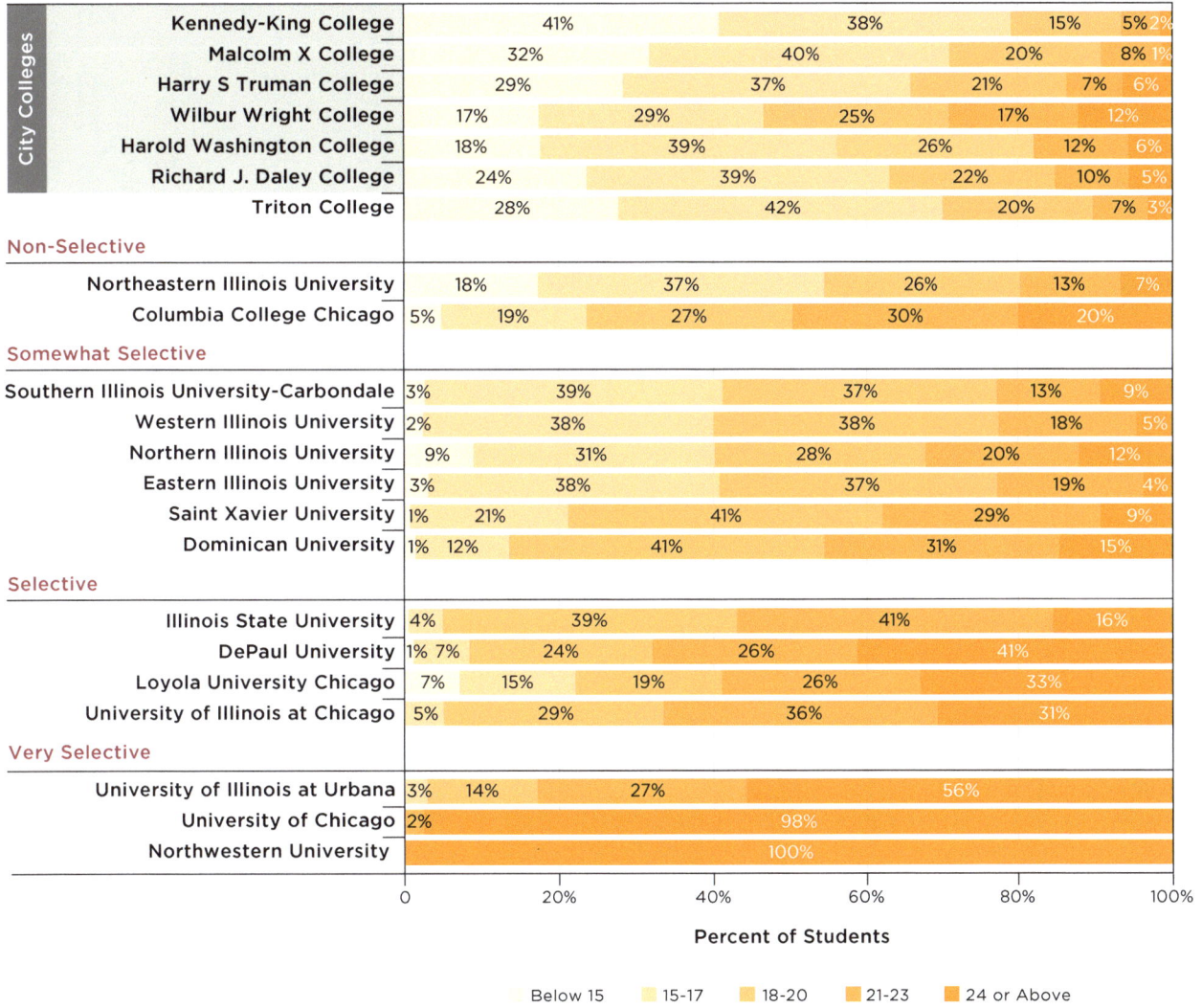

City Colleges					
Kennedy-King College	41%	38%	15%	5%	2%
Malcolm X College	32%	40%	20%	8%	1%
Harry S Truman College	29%	37%	21%	7%	6%
Wilbur Wright College	17%	29%	25%	17%	12%
Harold Washington College	18%	39%	26%	12%	6%
Richard J. Daley College	24%	39%	22%	10%	5%
Triton College	28%	42%	20%	7%	3%

Non-Selective

Northeastern Illinois University	18%	37%	26%	13%	7%
Columbia College Chicago	5% 19%	27%	30%	20%	

Somewhat Selective

Southern Illinois University-Carbondale	3% 39%	37%	13%	9%	
Western Illinois University	2% 38%	38%	18%	5%	
Northern Illinois University	9% 31%	28%	20%	12%	
Eastern Illinois University	3% 38%	37%	19%	4%	
Saint Xavier University	1% 21%	41%	29%	9%	
Dominican University	1% 12%	41%	31%	15%	

Selective

Illinois State University	4% 39%	41%	16%		
DePaul University	1% 7% 24%	26%	41%		
Loyola University Chicago	7% 15%	19%	26%	33%	
University of Illinois at Chicago	5% 29%	36%	31%		

Very Selective

University of Illinois at Urbana	3% 14%	27%	56%		
University of Chicago	2% 98%				
Northwestern University	100%				

0   20%   40%   60%   80%   100%

Percent of Students

Below 15   15-17   18-20   21-23   24 or Above

Note: Percentages do not include students missing ACT scores. Percentages may not add up to 100 due to rounding. Data and methods are described in Appendix A.

Earlier in this report (**see box "Delayed College Enrollment" on p.8**), we addressed delayed enrollment in college and highlighted how focusing exclusively on immediate entry to college masks broader patterns. Similarly, focusing only on students' initial college of post-secondary entry ignores the dynamic nature of the modern student's college career—an issue familiar to those in higher education, but perhaps less familiar to those in the K-12 sector. Here, we highlight CPS graduates' who enrolled in two-year *and* four-year colleges at some point in time. This approach captures students who transfer across levels of institutions, including students who delay college enrollment. The result provides a distinctly different story from initial immediate enrollment, one that uncovers a pattern of enrollment that involves two-year colleges as much as it does four-year colleges.

In **Figure A** (**see p.8**), we reported that 37 percent and 20 percent of 2009 CPS high school graduates immediately enrolled in four-year and two-year colleges, respectively. As shown in **Figure B**, however, we find that six years after graduating from high school, roughly the same number of 2009 high school graduates had enrolled at some point in a four-year college (48 percent) as had enrolled at some point in a two-year college (47 percent). Furthermore, as the cumulative percentage of graduates who enrolled in college increased 7 percentage points between 2006 and 2009, more than half of that growth was due to students who enrolled only in a two-year college.

Moreover, 19 percent of 2009 CPS graduates enrolled in both a four-year and a two-year college at some point over the course of six years, a number that is consistent over time. And about one-quarter of 2009 CPS high school graduates did not enroll in any level of college within six years of graduation, a number that has been declining over time. **Figure B** does not reflect the full extent of the enrollment and transfer phenomenon. For example, some students may start at a four-year college and then transfer to another, or start at a two-year college and take a couple of semesters off before resuming enrollment. However, there is a substantial set of CPS graduates that intersect with both two-year and four-year institutions.

FIGURE B

Three in Four CPS Graduates Enrolled in College Within Six Years of Graduating High School

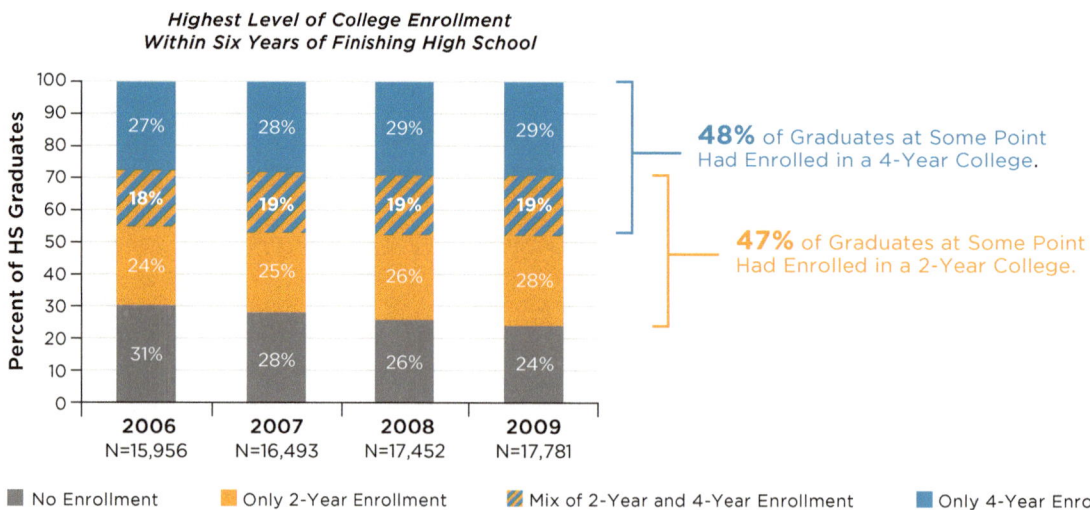

Highest Level of College Enrollment Within Six Years of Finishing High School

48% of Graduates at Some Point Had Enrolled in a 4-Year College.

47% of Graduates at Some Point Had Enrolled in a 2-Year College.

	2006 N=15,956	2007 N=16,493	2008 N=17,452	2009 N=17,781
Only 4-Year Enrollment	27%	28%	29%	29%
Mix of 2-Year and 4-Year Enrollment	18%	19%	19%	19%
Only 2-Year Enrollment	24%	25%	26%	28%
No Enrollment	31%	28%	26%	24%

■ No Enrollment ■ Only 2-Year Enrollment ▨ Mix of 2-Year and 4-Year Enrollment ■ Only 4-Year Enrollment

Note: Ns listed above refer to the number of high school graduates for each year. Percentages may not add up to 100 due to rounding. Data and methods are described in Appendix A.

Looking more closely at transfers, seen in **Figure C**, 26 percent of 2009 CPS graduates who immediately enrolled in a four-year college transferred to a two-year college at some point within four years (1,702 of 6,574 immediate four-year enrollees transferred to a two-year college). Of students who made an immediate transition to a two-year college, 16 percent transferred to a four-year college within four years (564 of 3,523 immediate two-year enrollees transferred to a four-year college). Students may have transferred to an institution of a different level and then transferred back to a college of their original level. Still, students who started at a four-year college were more likely to transfer to a two-year institution than students who started at a two-year institution were to transfer to a four-year institution.

FIGURE C

One in Four CPS Graduates Who First Enrolled in a Four-Year College Transferred to a Two-Year College Within Four Years of Graduating High School

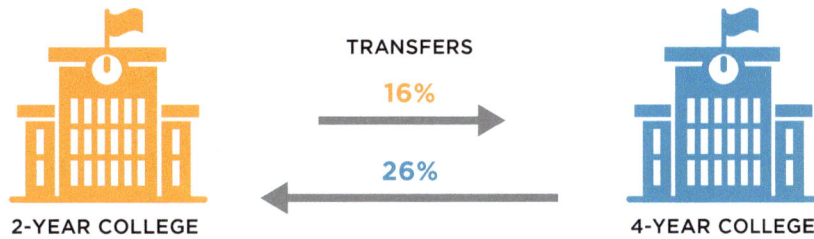

TRANSFERS

16%

26%

2-YEAR COLLEGE   4-YEAR COLLEGE

Note: Data and methods are described in Appendix A.

CHAPTER 4

Interpretive Summary

The college enrollment patterns identified in this report raise some key questions for policy and practice and lay the groundwork for our future research agenda on college access and success in Chicago. This research agenda can identify what is driving these patterns, as well as what high schools and colleges can do to support students' transition to post-secondary education and to improve their likelihood of success throughout college.

Implications for Policy and Practice

College enrollment extends long beyond the fall after graduation. A critical finding from this report is that college enrollment does not always fit into traditional timelines for CPS graduates. For example, close to a fifth of 2009 CPS graduates did not enroll in college the fall after graduation, but did eventually enroll within six years of high school graduation. Moreover, more than a quarter of the CPS graduates who immediately enrolled in a four-year college later transferred to a two-year college. And 16 percent of immediate two-year enrollees transferred to a four-year institution. These findings suggest that if we only pay attention to the students who make the immediate transition to college after high school graduation, and if we assume that these students stay in their institutions, we are losing sight of, and insights about, a sizable number of students. From research, policy, and practice perspectives, we need to build a more nuanced understanding of where and when students are enrolling in college.

Gaps in support during the college enrollment and choice processes still exist. The enrollment patterns of several different groups of students raise questions about gaps in support for college planning. There were significant percentages of CPS graduates who delayed entry into college, and significant percentages of CPS graduates who transferred between four-year and two-

year colleges. There were also nearly 1,000 students (959, or 19 percent) who graduated with a GPA of 3.0, but did not immediately enroll (the numbers are similar for students with ACT scores of 21 and above). There could be many reasons for these students not enrolling—and students may be making sound choices based on their situations—but these numbers raise questions about the supports these students were receiving. What would lead a student to transfer from a four-year college to a two-year college? What might prevent a student with a 3.0 GPA from immediately enrolling in a four-year college? How can practitioners adapt their student supports in light of this data?

CPS graduates who enroll in four-year colleges, enroll in two-year colleges, and don't enroll in college are more similar than we think. Though we often think of CPS students as self-selecting into different tiers of institutions, the data in this report suggest that there is considerable overlap in the students most local institutions serve. With the exception of a few very selective colleges, the vast majority of two-year and four-year colleges served CPS students with between a 2.0 and 3.0 GPA and a 15-20 ACT score. Many non-enrollees also fell into those categories. This has implications for how we think about supporting students with moderate qualifications in choosing whether to enroll in a two-year college, a four-year college, or any college at all.

Higher education institutions serve similar students; they could learn from and collaborate with each other. The overlap between groups of students also has implications for how institutions work together. A decade ago, collaboration among practitioners across high schools was sometimes viewed with skepticism because of the belief that different schools served different populations of students and did not have much to learn from each other. However, organizations like the Network for College Success and Umoja Student Development Corporation looked at the data and saw that, in fact, most high schools served a significant portion of students "in the middle"—students with average GPA, attendance, and test scores in eighth grade. Similarly, the data in this report suggests that seemingly different colleges like DePaul, Columbia, and Daley could learn from each other about strategies to successfully serve moderately qualified students. Opportunities for higher education institutions to share learning have gained momentum with the development of the Chicago Collaborative for Undergraduate Success, Thrive Chicago's college access change network, the Partnership for College Completion, and the Chicago Higher Education Compact. Findings in this report suggest that, when done well, cross-institution learning could be even more relevant than thought at first glance.

Chicago's comparatively high four-year enrollment rate is reason for celebration; continued improvement will require a two-pronged approach. Chicago's four-year college enrollment rate, as compared to the rates for other urban school districts, is certainly unusual. All the attention Chicago paid to college enrollment over the past decade has led to one of the highest four-year college enrollment rates for large urban districts. As CPS has continued to produce more graduates—and more highly-qualified graduates—the city of Chicago has built a robust infrastructure to help students make the transition to college. While there is clearly reason for celebration, enrollment is only the first step to a college degree. Research has demonstrated that college completion is shaped by students' academic prepara-

tion, particularly having at least a 3.0 GPA.[62] The 2015 four-year college enrollment rates mirrored the percentage of students who graduated with a 3.0 GPA or above. Efforts to help more students meet their educational aspirations need to use a two-pronged approach: they must continue to emphasize both 1) improving students' academic preparation for college, and 2) guiding students through the college application and college choice process. Increasing four-year college enrollment without ensuring that students are academically prepared does not put students in a position where they can succeed in college.

Implications for Future Research

How do students decide to enroll in four-year versus two-year colleges, or not enroll at all? CPS has achieved dramatic improvements in four-year college enrollment rates. Much could be learned about how district policies and school practices led to more students making the transition to four-year colleges. However, some students still delayed entry or did not enroll in college at all, including students with similar qualifications. Latino students, in particular, were disproportionately likely to enroll in two-year colleges in comparison to their White, Asian, and Black peers. To ensure that more students are considering their full range of options and are making college choices that reflect their interests and needs, it will be critical to know how students are deciding whether to enroll and which college to enroll in. In this report, we saw dramatic differences in patterns of two-year and four-year enrollment by type of high school attended. It is unclear if these patterns are being driven by the guidance provided by these high schools, students' financial, family or other constraints, or if these are fully informed decisions. Previous Consortium research showed that students of all qualification levels struggle at key points in the college enrollment process.[63] Research can provide practitioners further guidance on how to better support students at key college decision points (e.g., application and acceptance) and how to prevent "summer melt" between high school graduation and college enrollment.

---

62 Klasik (2012); Roderick et al. (2006); Roderick et al. (2008); Roderick et al. (2011).

63 Roderick et al. (2008); Roderick et al. (2011).

We also showed in this report that while Chicago's four-year college enrollment rates mirrored national rates, two-year college enrollment rates in Chicago were lower, including compared to other districts around the country. What is driving these lower rates? Is it the availability of a range of four-year college options in the Chicagoland area, is something different about the choice process or guidance CPS students receive, or is it something else?

Who succeeds at what kinds of colleges? What kinds of supports help students make a successful transition? What is the role of college costs and financial aid? In this report, we described the college enrollment patterns at two-year colleges and four-year colleges. But we have not yet examined whether these patterns reflect choices that give students a high likelihood of success in college. Previous research has demonstrated the importance of college choice, particularly the advantage gained by enrolling in colleges with high institutional graduation rates, but practitioners and families need help in knowing how to provide more nuanced and customized guidance to students so that they make college choices that maximize their likelihood of success. In the next stage of research, it will be critical to examine how academic preparation in high school and student characteristics are related to positive outcomes at colleges of varying selectivity levels, programs within colleges, and other college characteristics (e.g., cost and academic advising).

It will be equally important to further investigate how students' likelihood of success is shaped by their experiences once they reach college campuses. Colleges serving similar students often have very different graduation rates and different rates of transferring to other institutions.[64] Research can illuminate the practices, characteristics, and structures that support students through graduation. A better understanding of the role higher education plays in supporting students to graduation is critical so that more students have access to college options that give them a high probability of attaining a degree or credential.

Previous Consortium research has depended on the National Student Clearinghouse data to study post-secondary outcomes. However, these data only provide enrollment and completion for two-year colleges and four-year colleges, and lack more detailed information on whether students completed basic certificates, advanced certificates, or associate degrees at two-year colleges. We are hopeful that the availability of two-year outcome data through the Illinois Longitudinal Data System will soon provide insight on two-year completion type, as well as on other critical outcomes such as credit accumulation and enrollment in developmental or remedial courses.

How does transfer between institutions and stopping out affect students' post-secondary outcomes? What is the role of college characteristics in this "swirl?" One of the key findings of this report is the complexity of college enrollment patterns. One-fifth of CPS graduates spent time in both two-year and four-year colleges. This number does not take account of students who started at a two-year or four-year college and transferred to another college from the same level, nor students who may have stopped out of college and then re-enrolled in the same college or level. To increase the college completion rates of CPS graduates, it will be critical that we examine the full extent of the patterns of swirl and the role of student and college characteristics in transfers, to better understand the impact of these patterns.

What has the impact of the City Colleges of Chicago's Star Scholarship and other recent initiatives been on enrollment patterns? What does the performance of the scholarship recipients look like? As the national policy discussions have been placing a greater emphasis on the role two-year colleges play in expanding access to higher education, City Colleges has undergone significant shifts in their structure and their accessibility—most notably through the Chicago Star Scholarship, which allows qualified CPS graduates to pursue an associate's degree at no cost. Two-year college enrollment rates in Chicago have lagged behind national rates for the

---

64 Engle & O'Brien (2007).

past ten years. With the attention being paid to Chicago's two-year colleges and their recent initiatives, it will be critical to study whether enrollment patterns change, and if the initiatives are leading to improved completion rates for certificates and associate's degrees, as well as transfer to four-year colleges.

Conclusion

College enrollment is a critical transition for students. CPS has made impressive gains in college enrollment rates over the last decade, particularly in four-year college enrollment. Ultimately, however, the goal is to have more students graduate from college with credentials that can open doors to greater opportunity. For high schools, the challenge ahead is to prepare more students academically so that more of their graduates are positioned to succeed in college. For colleges, the challenge is to effectively support students once they reach college campuses so that they attain a college credential. While research can play a strong role in illuminating promising strategies and interventions, many high schools and colleges are already making strides. Sharing knowledge and supporting those working in high schools and colleges in their efforts to support students is an essential element in increasing the number of students who make it to and through college.

References

ACT, Inc. (2015)
College choice report 2015. Iowa City, IA: ACT.

Adelman, C. (2005)
Moving into town–and moving on: The community college in the lives of traditional-age students. Washington, DC: U.S. Department of Education.

Allensworth, E.M., Healey, K., Gwynne, J.A., & Crespin, R. (2016a)
High school graduation rates through two decades of district change: The influence of policies, data records, and demographic shifts. Chicago, IL: University of Chicago Consortium on School Research.

Allensworth, E.M., Moore, P.T., Sartain, L., & de la Torre, M. (2016b)
The educational benefits of attending higher performing schools. *Educational Evaluation and Policy Analysis. 20*(10), 1-23.

Bailey, M.J., & Dynarski, S.M. (2011)
Gains and gaps: Changing inequality in U.S. college entry and completion. NBER Working Paper 17633. Cambridge, MA: National Bureau of Economic Research. Retrieved from http://www.nber.org/papers/w17633

Barron's College Division. (2016)
Profiles of American colleges 2017. Hauppauge, NY: Barron's Educational Series.

Barrow, L., Sartain, L., & de la Torre, M. (2016)
The role of selective high schools in equalizing educational outcomes: Heterogeneous effects by neighborhood socioeconomic status. Working Paper. Chicago, IL: University of Chicago Consortium on School Research.

Berkner, L.K., He, S., & Cataldi, E.F. (2002)
Descriptive summary of 1995–96: Beginning post-secondary students six years later. (NCES 2003-151). U.S. Department of Education. Washington, DC: National Center for Education Statistics.

Bowen, W.G., Chingos, M.M., & McPherson, M.S. (2009)
Crossing the finish line: Completing college at America's public universities. Princeton, NJ: Princeton University Press.

Bozick, R., & DeLuca, S. (2005)
Better late than never? Delayed enrollment in the high school to college transition. *Social Forces, 84*(1), 531-554.

Buchmann, C., DiPrete, T.A., & McDaniel, A. (2008)
Gender inequalities in education. *Annual Review of Sociology, 34*, 319-37.

Carnevale, A.P., Jayasundera, T., & Hanson, A.R. (2012).
Career and technical education: Five ways that pay along the way to the BA. Washington, DC: Georgetown University Center on Education and the Workforce.

Cho, D. (2007)
The role of high school performance in explaining women's rising college enrollment. *Economics of Education Review, 26*(4), 450-462.

College Board. (2016a)
Trends in student aid: 2016. New York, NY: The College Board.

College Board. (2016b)
Table 8: Federal Pell Grants in current and constant (2015) dollars, 1973-74 to 2015-16 (web only table). New York, NY: The College Board. Retrieved from https://trends.collegeboard.org/student-aid/figures-tables/federal-pell-award-current-constant-dollars-over-time

Coca, V. (2014)
New York City goes to college: A first look at patterns of college enrollment, persistence, and degree attainment for NYC high school students. New York City, NY: The Research Alliance for New York City Schools.

DePaoli, J.L., Balfanz, R., & Bridgeland, J. (2016)
Building a grad nation: Progress and challenge in raising high school graduation rate. Baltimore, MD: Civic Enterprises: Everyone Graduates Center at the School of Education at Johns Hopkins University.

Dettro, C. (2015, August 13)
Local colleges crediting students for MAP grants held up by state budget impasse. *The State Journal-Register.* Retrieved from http://www.sj-r.com/article/20150813/NEWS/150819767

DiPrete, T.A., & Buchmann, C. (2014)
Gender disparities in educational attainment in the new century: Trends, causes and consequences. In J.R. Logan (Ed.), *Diversity and disparities: America enters a new century* (pp. 375-414). New York, NY: Russell Sage Foundation.

Durham, R.E., Ruiz, R., & Connolly, F. (2017)
Baltimore city schools college fact book. Baltimore, MD: Baltimore Education Research Consortium.

Engle, J., & O'Brien, C. (2007)
Demography is not destiny: Increasing the graduation rates of low-income college students at large public universities. Washington, DC: Pell Institute.

Fry, R. (2009)
College enrollment hits all-time high, fueled by community college surge. Washington, DC: Pew Research Center Publications.

Fry, R. (2011)
Hispanic college enrollment spikes, narrowing gaps with other groups. Washington, DC: Pew Hispanic Center.

Geiger, K. (2015, December 28)
State without a budget: Slow-motion mess in Illinois. *Chicago Tribune.* Retrieved from http://www.chicagotri-bune.com/news/local/politics/ct-illinois-budget-impasse-met-20151227-story.html

Goldin, C., Katz, L.F., & Kuziemko, I. (2006)
The homecoming of American college women: The reversal of the college gender gap. *The Journal of Economic Perspectives, 20*(4), 133-156.

Gwynne, J., & Moore, P.T. (forthcoming)
Chicago's charter high schools organizational features, enrollment, transfers, retention, and student performance. Chicago, IL: University of Chicago Consortium on School Research.

Hall, L.S. (2015)
Postsecondary outcomes of Dallas ISD graduates. Dallas, TX: Dallas Independent School District. Retrieved from https://www.dallasisd.org/cms/lib/TX01001475/Centricity/Domain/98/Evaluation/14-15/AtaGlance/EA15-107-04-At-a-Glance-Postsecondary.pdf

Healey, K., Nagaoka, J., & Michelman, V. (2014)
The educational attainment of Chicago public schools students: A focus on four-year college degrees. Chicago, IL: University of Chicago Consortium on Chicago School Research.

Hearn, J.C. (1991)
Academic and nonacademic influences on the college destinations of 1980 high school graduates. *Sociology of Education, 64*(3), 158-171.

Horn, L., Cataldi, E.F., & Sikora, A. (2005)
Waiting to attend college. undergraduates who delay their post-secondary enrollment. (NCES 2005-152). U.S. Department of Education. Washington, DC: National Center for Education Statistics.

Hurwitz, M., & Kumar, A. (2015)
Supply and demand in the higher education market: College admission and college choice. New York, NY: College Board.

Illinois Student Assistance Commission. (2012)
Monetary award program: Task force report. Springfield, IL: Illinois Student Assistance Commission. Retrieved from https://www.isac.org/about-isac/monetary-award-program-MAP-task-force/documents/MAPTaskForceReport-2012.pdf

Jones, B. (2016)
Two-thirds of L.A. Unified grads heading to college; growing number are university bound. [Press Release]. Los Angeles, CA: Los Angeles Unified School District. Retrieved from http://lausddaily.net/2016/05/two-thirds-of-l-a-unified-grads-heading-to-college-growing-number-are-university-bound/

Karen, D. (2002)
Changes in access to higher education in the United States: 1980-1992. *Sociology of Education, 75*(3), 191-210.

Kena, G., Hussar, W., McFarland, J., de Brey, C., Musu-Gillette, L., Wang, X., . . . Dunlop Velez, E. (2016)
The condition of education 2016. (NCES 2016-144). U.S. Department of Education. Washington, DC: National Center for Education Statistics. Retrieved from https://nces.ed.gov/pubs2016/2016144.pdf

Klasik, D. (2012)
The college application gauntlet: A systematic analysis of the steps to four-year college enrollment. *Research in Higher Education, 53*(5), 506-549.

Kurlaender, M. (2006)
Choosing community college: Factors affecting Latino college choice. *New Directions for Community Colleges, 2006*(133), 7-16.

McDonough, P.M. (1997)
Choosing colleges: How social class and schools structure opportunity. Albany, NY: State University of New York Press.

McFarland, J., Hussar, B., de Brey, C., Snyder, T., Wang, X., Wilkinson-Flicker, S., . . . Hinz, S. (2017)
The condition of education 2017 (NCES 2017- 144). U.S. Department of Education. Washington, DC: National Center for Education Statistics. Retrieved from https://nces.ed.gov/pubsearch/pubsinfo.asp?pubid=2017144

Mullins, C.M., & Phillippe, K. (2009)
Community college enrollment surge: An analysis of estimated fall 2009 headcount enrollments at community colleges. Washington, DC: American Association of Community Colleges.

Nagaoka, J., & Healey, K. (2016)
The educational attainment of Chicago Public Schools students, 2015: A focus on four-year college degrees. Chicago, IL: University of Chicago Consortium on School Research.

National Student Clearinghouse Research Center. (2016)
2016 high school benchmarks report. Herndon, VA: National Student Clearinghouse.

O'Connor, N. (2009)
Hispanic origin, socio-economic status, and community college enrollment. *The Journal of Higher Education, 80*(2), 121-145.

Perna, L.W. (2000)
Racial and ethnic group differences in college enroll-ment decisions. *New Directions for Institutional Research, 2000*(107), 65-83.

Reardon, S.F., Baker, R., & Klasik, D. (2012)
Race, income, and enrollment patterns in highly selective colleges, 1982-2004. Stanford, CA: Center for Education Policy Analysis, Stanford University.

Roderick, M., Coca, V., & Nagaoka, J. (2011)
Potholes on the road to college: High school effects in shaping urban students' participation in college applica-tion, four-year college enrollment, and college match. *Sociology of Education, 84*(3), 178-211.

Roderick, M., Nagaoka, J., Allensworth, E., Stoker, G., Correa, M., & Coca, V. (2006)
From high school to the future: A first look at Chicago Public Schools graduates: College enrollment, college preparation, and graduation from four-year colleges. Chicago, IL: University of Chicago Consortium on Chicago School Research.

Roderick, M., Nagaoka, J., Coca, V., & Moeller, E. (2008)
From high school to the future: Potholes on the road to college. Chicago, IL: University of Chicago Consortium on Chicago School Research.

Roderick, M., Nagaoka, J., Coca, V., & Moeller, E. (2009)
From high school to the future: making hard work pay off: The road to college for students in CPS' academically advanced programs. Chicago, IL: University of Chicago Consortium on Chicago School Research.

Smith, J., Pender, M., Howell, J., & Hurwitz, M. (2012)
The CollegeKeys Compact™. Getting into college: Post-secondary academic undermatch. New York, NY: College Board.

Turner, S. (2004)
Going to college and finishing college. Explaining different educational outcomes. In C.M. Hoxby (Ed.), *College choices: The economics of where to go, when to go, and how to pay for it* (pp. 13-62). Chicago, IL: University of Chicago Press.

Woodhouse, K. (2016, January 7)
Universities left footing the bill as budget crisis looms in Illinois. *Inside Higher Ed.* Retrieved from https://www.insidehighered.com/news/2016/01/07/universities-left-footing-bill-budget-crisis-looms-illinois

Appendix A
Data and Methods

Data Sources

Information on student demographics, ACT scores, course grades, and high school graduation is from CPS administrative records, which are shared with the UChicago Consortium through its Master Research Services agreement with the district. All data are available for charter school students, with the exception of course grades used to compute GPAs (**see "GPA and Course Grades" for more details**).

Data from the National Student Clearinghouse (NSC) are used for all college enrollment rates. The NSC houses records on enrollment and post-secondary credentials for colleges throughout the United States, and covers 98 percent of all post-secondary enrollments nationally. Selectivity categories are based on ratings from *Barron's Profiles of American Colleges* (2016). All of these data are available for charter school graduates.

The Census's American Community Survey (ACS) served as an additional source of information for this report. Specifically, Census block-group level information from 2012 (e.g., median family income in 2012 dollars) was linked to students' residential information as a proxy for a student's family income level.

Data Definitions

College Enrollment

For most of this report, the college enrollment rate is the proportion of graduates who immediately enrolled in a post-secondary institution (which participates in the NSC) in the *fall following high school graduation*. Students who graduated from special education schools or alternative diploma programs are not counted as graduates. Graduates who enroll in primarily baccalaureate degree-granting institutions are considered four-year enrollees; graduates who enroll in institutions that primarily grant associate's degrees or certificates are considered two-year college enrollees. Off-cycle graduates are counted as graduates in the school year

in which they graduated. To compare enrollment rates by high school type, graduates are assigned to the high school where they were enrolled in the spring of their graduation year, or their last active school for off-cycle graduates. Graduates are not identified as college enrollees either if they enroll in colleges that do not report enrollment data to the NSC, or if they request that their college not share their data with the NSC.

Individual schools may have better data on their graduates' college enrollment. The NSC relies on a matching algorithm to pair data provided by CPS on their graduates with data provided by colleges. This algorithm may produce different results using data provided by schools, which may be more current than the data given by CPS. Additionally, schools may have other evidence (e.g., course schedules or transcripts) of their graduates' college enrollment.

Delayed College Enrollment

Delayed enrollment includes matriculation into a two- or four-year institution subsequent the fall after high school graduation but within six years of graduating high school. Delayed college enrollment only includes the institution where students began their college career, not any subsequent transfers.

Overall Enrollment Patterns Six Years Out

The **"Overall Enrollment Patterns Six Years Out" box on p.20** includes students' enrollment in college at any time within six years of high school graduation (includes immediate enrollees, delayed enrollees, and transfers between levels of institution).

ACT Composite Score

ACT score is the composite score students received when they took the ACT as part of the Prairie State Achievement Examination taken by all eleventh-graders in the state of Illinois. These statistics are likely underestimates of CPS students' performance submitted in college applications because they do not reflect the higher scores that students who retake the exam may have submitted to colleges. These statistics differ from those published by CPS because they reflect the scores of graduates and not the scores of all students who take the ACT. The state of Illinois switched from the ACT to the SAT in 2017.

GPA and Course Grades

GPA is the cumulative, unweighted average of grades received in core courses (English, math, science, and social studies) at graduation. Only GPAs based on four or more semester credits are included. Many CPS charter schools use different student information systems from the IMPACT system used by non-charter schools. Because each system varies in the way that it stores information about courses, credits, teachers, periods, grades, and other data, creating linkages across systems is a difficult, and our data archive currently does not include records of charter school students' course performance. We are therefore unable to include charter school students in GPA analyses. Charter school students constituted 17 percent of 2015 graduates.

ABOUT THE AUTHORS

VANESSA M. COCA is an independent research consultant for the UChicago Consortium with extensive experience conducting research on post-secondary transitions of public school students in Chicago and New York City. As an Institute of Education Sciences (IES) pre-doctoral research fellow at the Research Alliance for New York City Schools—a research center housed at New York University (NYU)—Coca developed a massive longitudinal database to track the college transitions of all New York City (NYC) public school students and supported the NYC Partnership for College Readiness and Success, a research-practitioner partnership between the City University of New York City, the NYC Department of Education, and the Research Alliance. She is the lead author of *New York City Goes to College: A First Look at Patterns of College Enrollment, Persistence, and Degree Attainment for NYC Students* (2014), the Alliance's inaugural report that examined trends in college enrollment, persistence, and completion utilizing this longitudinal database.

Prior to her work at the Alliance, Coca worked as a Senior Research Analyst at the UChicago Consortium as part of the Chicago post-secondary transitions project, where she contributed to a series of highly regarded reports on CPS students' transitions to college. Coca received a BA and a master's degree in public policy from the University of Chicago. She is currently a doctoral candidate in the sociology of education program at the Steinhardt School of Culture, Education, and Human Development at NYU.

JENNY NAGAOKA is the Deputy Director of the UChicago Consortium, where she has conducted research for nearly 20 years. Her research interests focus on policy and practice in urban education reform, particularly using data to connect research and practice and examining the school environments and instructional practices that promote college readiness and success. She has co-authored numerous journal articles and reports, including studies of college readiness, noncognitive factors, the transition from high school to post-secondary education, and authentic intellectual instruction. She is the lead researcher on the To&Through Project, a project that provides educators, policymakers, and families with research, data, and training on the milestones that matter most for college success. Nagaoka is the lead author of *Foundations for Young Adult Success: A Developmental Framework* (2015), which draws on research and practice evidence to build a coherent framework of the foundational factors for young adult success, and investigates their development from early childhood through young adulthood and how they can be supported through developmental experiences and relationships.

Nagaoka received her BA from Macalester College and her master's degree in public policy from the Irving B. Harris School of Public Policy at the University of Chicago.

ALEX SEESKIN is the Chief Strategy Officer at the University of Chicago Urban Education Institute (UEI), where he is responsible for guiding strategy for organizing and leading high-priority work across and within UEI's units. Seeskin also leads the To&Through Project (toandthrough.uchicago. edu), which aims to empower educators and families with the research, data, and resources they need to move more students to and through high school and college. Previously, he served as the Director of Strategy of UChicago Charter and as a resident at UChicago Impact.

Prior to coming to UEI, Seeskin taught high school English in Chicago Public Schools for seven years, serving as the English department chair at Lake View High School from 2008–12. Seeskin earned a BS in communications from Northwestern University and an EdLD from Harvard University.

UCHICAGO Consortium
on School Research

Directors

ELAINE M. ALLENSWORTH
Lewis-Sebring Director

STACY EHRLICH
*Managing Director and
Senior Research Scientist*

JULIA A. GWYNNE
*Managing Director and
Senior Research Scientist*

HOLLY HART
Survey Director

KYLIE KLEIN
*Director of Research
Operations*

BRONWYN MCDANIEL
*Director of Outreach
and Communication*

JENNY NAGAOKA
Deputy Director

MELISSA RODERICK
*Senior Director
Hermon Dunlap Smith
Professor
School of Social Service
Administration*

PENNY BENDER SEBRING
Co-Founder

MARISA DE LA TORRE
*Managing Director and
Senior Research Associate*

Steering Committee

RAQUEL FARMER-HINTON
Co-Chair
University of Wisconsin,
Milwaukee

DENNIS LACEWELL
Co-Chair
Urban Prep Charter Academy
for Young Men

Ex-Officio Members

SARA RAY STOELINGA
Urban Education Institute

Institutional Members

SARAH DICKSON
Chicago Public Schools

ELIZABETH KIRBY
Chicago Public Schools

TROY LARAVIERE
Chicago Principals and
Administrators Association

KAREN G.J. LEWIS
Chicago Teachers Union

ALAN MATHER
Chicago Public Schools

TONY SMITH
Illinois State
Board of Education

Individual Members

GINA CANEVA
Lindblom Math & Science

NANCY CHAVEZ
City Colleges of Chicago

KATIE HILL
Office of the Cook County
State's Attorney

MEGAN HOUGARD
Chicago Public Schools

GREG JONES
Kenwood Academy

PRANAV KOTHARI
Revolution Impact, LLC

LILA LEFF
Umoja Student Development
Corporation & Emerson
Collective

RITO MARTINEZ
Surge Institute

LUISIANA MELÉNDEZ
Erikson Institute

SHAZIA MILLER
NORC at the
University of Chicago

CRISTINA PACIONE-ZAYAS
Erikson Institute

BEATRIZ PONCE DE LEÓN
Generation All

PAIGE PONDER
One Million Degrees

**KATHLEEN ST. LOUIS
CALIENTO**
The Academy Group

AMY TREADWELL
Chicago New Teacher Center

**REBECCA VONDERLACK-
NAVARO**
Latino Policy Forum

PAM WITMER
Illinois Network of
Charter Schools

JOHN ZEIGLER
DePaul University

www.ingramcontent.com/pod-product-compliance
Lightning Source LLC
LaVergne TN
LVHW072121070426
835511LV00002B/50